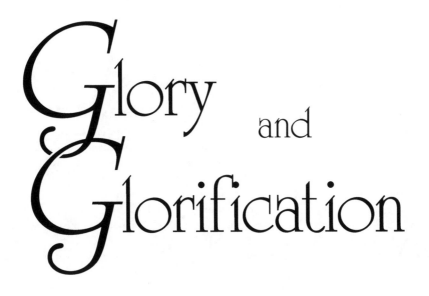

Glory and Glorification

BIBLICAL REFLECTIONS

Ross Kingwell, Ph.D.

WESTBOW
PRESS®
A DIVISION OF THOMAS NELSON
& ZONDERVAN

WestBow Press books may be ordered through booksellers or by contacting:

WestBow Press
A Division of Thomas Nelson & Zondervan
1663 Liberty Drive
Bloomington, IN 47403
www.westbowpress.com
1 (866) 928-1240

ISBN: 978-1-9736-8900-3 (sc)
ISBN: 978-1-9736-8901-0 (e)

Print information available on the last page.

WestBow Press rev. date: 3/25/2020

Contents

Abbreviations

ISV International Standard Version
KJV King James Version
NASB New American Standard Bible
NIV New International Version
JV New Jerusalem Bible or Jerusalem Version
NKJV New King James Version
Most quotations of biblical verses in this book are
from the NIV, unless otherwise indicated.

Preface

These notes are written somewhat sheepishly, almost out of embarrassment and follow years of ignorance.

It would make for a very long day if I were to list the number of times and occasions when I read or parroted the words *glory, glorify and glorification*, yet was nagged by awareness of my cursory comprehension of their meaning. Like letters in a Christian alphabet soup, these words swirled around to be sipped and enjoyed. They were part of the litany of ingredients of religious sustenance — but I was left with the after-taste of my scant knowledge of their character and core.

Of some comfort to me, when commencing to understand better the meaning of glory, was an on-line comment by David Reagan[1] where he bluntly said about glory: "It is one of those important words that is hard to explain". Like that writer, I knew the word *glory* was important, yet I also suspected that I might not be able easily to define it. Therefore, sensing a potentially difficult journey ahead, I ventured to design these notes and build my knowledge about *glory* and *glorification*; and thereby, at least, remove my regret at not commencing earlier.

Unfortunately, I am no biblical scholar or expert, so I've needed to draw on the comments and insights of a range of commentators and scholars to help provide me with a deeper appreciation of *glory* and *glorification* as stated in the Christian scriptures. I hope these notes feed the curiosity of readers who, like me, want elucidation of the words *glory, glorify* and

---

[1] (see http://www.learnthebible.org/what-is-glory.html [accessed March 12, 2020])

glorification as cited in the scriptures. To the extent that these notes enrich any person's walk with the Lord then their preparation has served a useful purpose.

Ross Kingwell, Ph.D.

Introduction

The word glory occurs 300 times in 279 verses in the New International Version (NIV) translation of the bible, 402 times in 371 verses in the King James Version (KJV) and 359 times in 331 verses in the New American Standard Bible (NASB). In addition, in the Old Testaments of these translations the word glory occurs 163 times in 154 verses in the NIV, 225 times in 214 verses in the KJV and 194 times in 185 verses in the NASB. Thus, the word glory is prevalent in both the Old and New Testaments.

The differences in word counts between translations reveal there is not always unanimity between scholars and linguistic experts as to when the English word glory should be selected to convey the meaning or nuance of the relevant Hebrew or Greek words in the source materials of these translations. For example, there are up to 12 Hebrew and Aramaic words that, depending on the textual circumstance and the leanings of the translators, are translated as the word glory and similarly there are nine Greek words translated as glory.

Grammatically, the word glory can be a noun or a verb. As a verb, glory usually means to boast, to praise, to revel in, to bask in, or be enthralled, enraptured or captivated. More frequently in the scriptures, glory is used as a noun. It is this use of the word glory, mostly as a noun, that is the focus of this book.

The fact that different translations of the Old and New Testaments at times differ over when to apply the word glory not only indicates a lack of unanimity in translation choice but also suggests glory has synonyms, or that there are other words or phrases that capture some similar or different nuance of the word glory. It is not always easy to capture the full meaning of a word in one language when translating that word into another language. In addition, as we know from English words, even the meaning of a word can change over time. However, due to the number and range of occurrences of use of the word glory in the scriptures (and from other ancient literature using the same root words), it is possible to form a reasonably accurate picture of what is conveyed or meant by the word glory as we read it in the English translations of the scriptures.

Unfortunately, no single verse fully and clearly spells out with precision what entirely is meant by the word glory. Hence, to garner an understanding of glory requires the study of many verses and passages that touch on aspects or illustrations of glory. Such diligent digging increases the likelihood of forming an accurate and fulsome view of the word glory as we read it in the scriptures.

God's Glory

The Old Testament

The main, most frequent Hebrew word translated as glory in the Old Testament is the Hebrew word kbd, transliterated into English as *kabowd* or *kavod* and more rarely *kabod*. Its pronunciation is similar to saying k-ahh-vode. The first syllable is a long, rounded "a" as in car or cart. The second syllable's sound rhymes with mode or rode; and the "b" is actually closer to a "v". Therefore, *kabowd* or *kabod* or *kavod* is pronounced k-ahh-vode. With this linguistic lesson over, let us press on.

The Hebrew word *kabowd* occurs 202 times in 191 verses in the Hebrew concordance of the NASB and 200 times in 189 verses in the Hebrew concordance of the KJV. The still popular KJV translates the Hebrew word *kabowd* in the following manner: glory (n=156), honour (n=32), glorious (n=10), gloriously (n=1) and honourable (n=1). The phrase "glory of the Lord" occurs 38 times in the NASB and 36 times in the KJV.

Characteristics of God's Glory

The Old Testament makes plain that where God is, is where His glory dwells (Psalm 26:8). Hence, the first characteristic to note about God's glory is that it is His property.

His Property

God's glory belongs to Him. Isaiah 42:8 states: "I am the Lord; that is my name! I will not give my glory to another or my praise to idols." God's glory, His magnificence, His greatness is His property — His alone. Although we receive and can reflect His glory, God remains the source of that glory. "Arise, shine, for your light has come, and the glory of the LORD rises upon you…..the LORD rises upon you and his glory appears over you." (Isaiah 60:1-2). We are created in "the image and glory of God" (1 Corinthians 11:7), "in the likeness of God" (Genesis 5:1) and at best we reflect His glory (e.g. Moses in the desert (Exodus 34:29), Moses and Elijah at the transfiguration (Luke 9:30-31)).

Visible, Splendorous and Powerful

Some of the first references to the glory of God in the Old Testament are references to the visibility of glory: "..in the morning you will see the glory of the LORD," (Exodus 16:7) and "While Aaron was speaking to the whole Israelite assembly, they looked toward the desert, and there was the glory of the LORD appearing in the cloud" (Exodus 16:10). This glory was a visual emanation of God's magnificence. Later in Exodus the glory of God is described as being "like consuming fire on the top of the mountain." (Exodus 24:17).

God's glory as emanations of light and fire recur throughout the bible, indicating that God is both splendorous, pure, holy and unapproachable, even in this mode of self-revelation. Later in Exodus is described how "Moses could not enter the Tent of Meeting because the cloud settled on it, and the glory of the LORD filled the tabernacle" (Exodus 40:35). Reflecting on his knowledge of these scriptures, later, the apostle Paul writes to Timothy, saying that God, "the King of kings and Lord of lords…..who lives in unapproachable light" (1 Timothy 6:15-16). Therefore, we learn from the Old Testament that God's glory is visible and splendorous, often in the form of cloud or fire. "They will see the glory of the LORD, the splendour of our God" (Isaiah 35:2). The glory of God is the manifestation of His presence, His splendour and magnificence.

God's glory is pure luminosity. God's glory illuminates and exposes. The apostle John, in the New Testament, acknowledges this by saying, "God is Light; in him there is no darkness at all." (1 John 1:5). Revelation 21:23 describes the New Jerusalem as a city that "does not need the sun or moon to shine on it, for the glory of the God gives it light." Revelation 21:10-11 also describes the city "coming down out of heaven from God. It shone with the glory of God, and its brilliance was like that of a very precious jewel, like a jasper, clear as crystal."

God's glory, as described in the Old Testament, can be visually, geographically constrained (e.g. "the glory of the Lord settled on Mount Sinai." (Exodus 24:16) or "the glory of the LORD filled the tabernacle" (Exodus 40:34)). However, God's glory can also be geographically unconstrained ("the *whole* earth is full of his glory" (Isaiah 6:3)) in the sense that the whole earth is full of His magnificence (also see Psalm 19:1-6).

God's glory is a display of His power and might. God's revealed glory is splendorous, but also powerful, synonymous with "a consuming fire". Such is the power of God's glory that the apostle Paul describes it as "unapproachable light" (1 Timothy 6:16). Its power is transformative, as illustrated by the effect of God's glory on Moses. When Moses drew near to God and spent time in the holiness of God's presence, Moses was visibly transformed — "When Moses came down from Mount Sinai with the two tablets of the Testimony in his hands, he was not aware that his face was radiant because he had spoken with the LORD." (Exodus 34:29). Similarly, with the Lord Jesus at the transfiguration —"As he was praying, the appearance of his face changed," (Luke 9:29). Matthew's account describes the same incident as "There he was transfigured before them. His face shone like the sun," (Matthew 17:2).

Although God's glory is powerful and capable of being transformative, it is not helpful nor valid to extrapolate from the transfiguration or Moses' interchange with God on Mount Sinai and suggest a product of prayer is that we will experience God's glory and be physically illuminated. That Moses and Christ were transfigured is true. However, there are many other instances where Christ and many other notable figures in the scriptures were in earnest prayer, yet no alteration in the brightness of their visage is noted to indicate a direct encounter of God's glory. Interchange with

God can alter much in a person, including their attitudes, behaviours and emotion but the physical mark of visible brightness is exceedingly rare, as evidenced by the very few times it is recorded in the scriptures. However, these few instances nonetheless do illustrate the power and transformative influence of God's glory.

In summary, thus far, God's glory is the manifestation of His greatness (Exodus 16:10) and is seen as a consuming fire (Exodus 24:17), a cloud (Numbers 16:42, 1 Kings 8:11), or fire within cloud (Exodus 40:38), radiance (Ezekiel 1:26-28), and brightness (Ezekiel 10:4). It can have specific geographical visibility such as atop Mount Sinai or filling the tabernacle (Exodus 40:34) or it can range widely such as "the *whole* earth is full of His glory" (Isaiah 6:3).

It is worth noting, in passing, that radiance is not solely associated with God's glory. Psalm 19:8b says, "The commands of the LORD are radiant, giving light to the eyes." In addition, Psalm 119:105 says, "Your word is a lamp to my feet and a light for my path."

Indicative of Great Worth, Abundance; and Worthy of Praise and Honour

Another learning from the Old Testament is that God's glory also is linked to honour, praise and worthiness. For the ancient Hebrews, the weight and importance of the LORD God was such that they saw and called Him the King of kabod (i.e. "the LORD Almighty — he is the King of glory" (Psalm 24:10)). The grandeur or weightiness of God's glory is not solely the display of His riches, as it may often be for an earthly king or ruler. Rather, the kabod of God is His great honour and dignity—His gravitas is accompanied by His splendour. His radiance is a display of His magnificence and power. God's glory is both His visible presence and His observable magnificence.

Importantly, God's splendour, being visible, shows His commitment to revelation. However, as discussed later in the section on the "New Testament", the display of God's glory, the visible manifestation of His presence, is not always accompanied by luminescence. His glory is revelatory and visible, but it is not always associated with dazzling, abundant luminosity.

The 18th century North American preacher, philosopher and theologian, Jonathan Edwards, notes that the Hebrew noun *Kavod* (sometimes *Kabod*) "signifies gravity, heaviness, greatness, and abundance." (p. 6, cited by Hickman (1840)). Edwards stresses that the glory of God speaks to His internal glory, signifying what is inherent within God and to the external expression or communication of that internal glory.

Edwards (1844) observes that God's glory involves emanation and remanation (return). He says, "The refulgence shines upon and into the creature, and is reflected back to the luminary. The beams of glory come from God and are something of God, and are refunded back to their original. So that the whole is *of* God, and *in* God, and to God; and God *is* the beginning, middle and end in the affair." (p. 255). Moses' interaction with God is one example of the enduring power of God's glory and ability to generate reflection. Exodus 34:29 recounts how Moses "was not aware that his face was radiant because he had spoken with the LORD." The after-glow was so striking that Aaron and all other Israelites were afraid to come near Moses (Exodus 34:30).

His Revelation

God's glory is visible. It reveals His presence. It is consistent with God being Revelation — "To the Israelites the glory of the LORD looked like a consuming fire on top of the mountain." (Exodus 24:17), indicating that God can, at various times, visibly reveal His presence.

The New Testament

In the New Testament, of the nine Greek words translated as glory, the most frequently used is δόξα or δόξαν anglicised as doxa or doxan. The word originates from the Greek verb δοκεῖν with the anglicised meanings of "to appear", "to seem", "to think" and "to accept". It was a Greek word for common belief or popular opinion. The value, weight or importance of something was often the product of popular opinion and belief. Doxa literally meant "what evokes good opinion or which has inherent, intrinsic worth." Between the third and first centuries BC, usage of the word doxa enlarged its meaning beyond valued popular opinion additionally to convey concepts of glory, honour, grandeur and importance. Hence, when the Septuagint translated the Hebrew word for glory (כבוד, kavod) as doxa, they were using the word to indicate the intrinsic worth, importance or heaviness of a person or God.

Use of the word doxa or doxan (i.e. δόξα or δόξαν) in the New Testament conveys a few meanings. Often it refers simply to good, favourable or high opinion given to or received by a person. Hence, praise and honour can be given or received. For example, due to their faithfulness to Christ (1 Thessalonians 1:3), Paul, Silas and Timothy, when writing to the church of the Thessalonians, could say of them, "you are our glory and joy" (1 Thessalonians 2:20). However, doxa or doxan (i.e. δόξα or δόξαν) in the New Testament can have other meanings. For example, Albert Barnes, in his commentary on Romans 2:7 says that "The word glory δόξαν denotes, properly, *praise, celebrity*, or anything distinguished for beauty, ornament, majesty, splendour, as of the sun, etc.; and then it is used to denote the highest happiness or felicity, as expressing everything that shall be splendid, rich and grand. It denotes that there will be an absence of everything *mean, grovelling, obscure*." (p. 560 in Barnes' Notes on the New Testament, 1962)

The Greek words δόξα (doxa) and δόξαν (doxan) have 37 and 58 occurrences respectively in the New Testament. The most frequent English translation of these Greek words is the word glory. However, other English words selected, when translating the word doxa, include glorious, honour, praise, dignity and worship.

The commentator Albert Barnes notes that when the classic writers used the word glory they were referring to (i) opinion, sentiment or (ii) fame, reputation or (iii) splendour and brightness. Hence, for example, in the Old Testament there are many Mosaic references to the radiance of God's glory. Yet, God's glory need not always be signposted by radiance or brightness, but rather by power. A notable example is when Jesus displayed His authority and power by changing water into wine (John 2:1-10). In describing this miraculous conversion, the apostle John writes: "He thus revealed his glory" (John 2:11). This miracle entailed no luminosity but rather the visible display of power, the manifestation and evidence of God's glory.

In the New Testament, Saint Paul's use of language regarding the word glory is worthy of examination. As his many letters reveal, he was highly skilled in the use of language. Firstly, he was thoroughly knowledgeable of Hebrew, the language and content of the Old Testament, due to his upbringing and education. As a child in Tarsus, he would have attended the Jewish school attached to the town's synagogue. There he would have listened to the hazzam or synagogue keeper and would have rote learned Hebrew phrases and their proper intonation. He would have learned to write all the Hebrew characters and would have practised copying parts of the ancient scriptures. Later, he was educated further in the use of Hebrew as a student in a pharisaic school under the tutelage of Gamaliel in Jerusalem. Paul says of himself, "Under Gamaliel I was thoroughly trained in the law of our fathers" (Acts 22:3). He later describes the Old Testament scriptures in his letter to the Romans (Romans 1:2) with the Greek words hagiais graphais (i.e. holy scriptures).

Secondly, Paul grew up in a Greek-speaking town, Tarsus in Cilicia (Acts 22:3). So, from a young age, Paul would have developed a familiarity and finesse in Greek and Hebrew. He would have been surrounded by the daily interaction of Greek speakers, whilst being taught Hebrew at the synagogue school. The tradition in Paul's era was that his father would have presented him the Septuagint (i.e. a Greek translation of the Old Testament) written on vellum, not papyrus.

Paul's skill in using Hebrew and Greek is revealed when dictating one of his letters to the church at Corinth, as he combined both Hebrew and Greek ideas in the term βάρος δόξης (i.e. translated into English as "weight of glory" (2 Corinthians 4:17)). It was an insightful and accurate word invention by him. Paul already would have been aware of the Hebrew meaning of *Kabod* (or *Kavod*) signifying "gravity, heaviness, greatness, and abundance". The Greek word βάρος which means weight, heaviness or burden accurately reflects this Hebrew word Kabod.

The entire Greek sentence containing the phrase βάρος δόξης is: "τὸ γὰρ παραυτίκα ἐλαφρὸν τῆς θλίψεως καθ' ὑπερβολὴν εἰς ὑπερβολὴν αἰώνιον βάρος δόξης κατεργάζεται ἡμῖν" (2 Corinthians 4:17). This is translated in the New American Standard Bible as, "For momentary, light affliction is producing for us an eternal weight of glory far beyond all comparison." In this verse the Greek phrase, βάρος means weight, heaviness or burden, whilst δόξης means glory. Hence, Paul captures elements of the Hebrew and Greek languages to convey the idea that Christ's followers will experience God's glory that reveals His heaviness, importance, or weightiness.

One of the clearest glimpses of God's glory in the New Testament is the glory of Christ, mentioned in the gospels in the narrative of the transfiguration. Thus, I want to examine in some detail, the biblical texts that describe the transfiguration.

Christ's Transfiguration

The transfiguration is reported in all the gospels, except John's. The absence of the story from John's gospel is surprising as he was one of the three disciples who witnessed the event. However, John is acutely aware of Christ's glory for he writes in his gospel "We have seen his glory, the glory of the one and only [Son]" (John 1:14). The writer of Hebrews supports this statement by the apostle John, saying of Christ: "The Son is the radiance of God's glory and the exact representation of his being, sustaining all things by his powerful word." (Hebrews 1:3). The apostle John in writing the Book of Revelation also records how, following the triumphant return of Christ and the establishment of a New Jerusalem, Christ is the lamp that lights this city (See Revelation 21:23).

The other gospels' references that specifically describe the transfiguration are Matthew 17:1-9, Mark 9:2-10 and Luke 9:28-36. Matthew writes that Christ was "transfigured before them" and "his face did shine as the sun, and his raiment was white as the light." Mark does not mention how Christ's face shone but does say that "his raiment became shining, exceeding white as snow; so as no fuller on earth can white them." Luke states, "as he prayed, the fashion of his countenance was altered, and his raiment was white and glistering."

As a possible aside for those not familiar with the occupation of a fuller (Mark 9:3) — a fuller was responsible for cleaning cloth, usually in preparation for its subsequent dyeing. Raw cloth first was cleansed of its natural oils and gums. Various cleansers were used, including white clay, urine, and the ashes of certain desert plants (see Malachi 3:2). The fuller's shop was often outside a city (2 Kings 18:17; Isaiah 7:3; 36:2), due to the space required for the airing of treated cloth and because of the stench of the urine treatment.

The Anglo-Saxon word fullian means "to whiten" and is the basis for the English word "full" as applied to cleansing cloth. In English, to full is to press or scour cloth. The trade of fullers, as mentioned in scripture, is mostly about cleansing and whitening garments. The process consisted of treading or stamping on the garments, with the feet or with bats, in tubs of water, in which mostly some alkaline substance like natron (Proverbs 25:20; Jeremiah 2:22) or soap (Malachi 3:2) was dissolved.

Hence, at the transfiguration, when Christ's clothing is described as the whiteness of pure snow, whiter than any fuller could achieve; it is stressing the vivid purity and brightness of its whiteness. In their assessment, it is not a manufactured brightness such as a fuller might achieve. It is a white glistering never encountered in their experience. It is real, powerful and utterly unusual.

The Greek word for transfigured, μεταμορφόω, is transliterated as metamorphoó. The English word metamorphosis is derived from this same Greek word. The word means to change radically. In the gospels, this transfiguration is a change, not in Jesus' nature, but is a transformation that makes visible His true self and essence. The verb only occurs four times in the New Testament (Mark 9:2; Matthew 17:2; Romans 12:2; 2 Corinthians 3:18). In each instance, a marked change or transformation is described.

Illuminating and novel though the transfiguration was, it is worth heeding the comments of the nineteenth century commentator Albert Barnes when he said, "The word transfiguration means to change the appearance or form. It does not denote the change of the substance of a thing, but simply of its appearance." The Lord Jesus Christ, from the beginning of time (John 1:2-4), through his earthly sojourn, and forevermore, is the Son of God; the righteous branch, the Lamb of God (Revelation 21:23). The transfiguration certainly changed His appearance but not His person, His substance. That was changeless.

The apostle John notes in his gospel that the disciples were not alone in glimpsing Christ's glory. The apostle John notes that Isaiah said his prophesies "because he saw Jesus' glory" and so "spoke about him." (John 12:37-41). John indicates that Isaiah was among the company of those that already had glimpsed or were aware of Jesus' glory. Isaiah's prophesies related to the nature of Christ and unbelief of many Jews in Him, despite His myriad of miracles.

Note that the transfigured (glorified) Christ, full of luminosity and radiating purity, was responsive to all; Moses, Elijah and the disciples. He was able to hear, understand, express, see, be moved, move, share and care. His countenance was changed but much was unchanged, such as His willingness and ability to interact, listen, speak, see, empathise and encourage.

By contrast, for the disciples, the experience of the transfiguration was novel and fearsome. The writer of Mark's gospel says of Peter "..he did not know what to answer; for they became terrified." (Mark 9:6, NASB). Other translations use similar words such as "sore afraid" (KJV), "frightened" (NIV) or in the Greek, literally "out of one's wits". So here, all three disciples were filled with terror and fear, and when Peter blurted out his keenness to erect shelters, so wrapped in fright was he, that he had no idea what he was actually saying. By contrast, the interaction with Christ by Moses and Elijah was empathetic, purposeful, engaging and lacking in terror. In short, Moses and Elijah were comfortable in the presence of the glorified Christ whereas the disciples were not. Later, in reflection, because he had witnessed the behaviour of Elijah and Moses, Peter would register that it was possible to be in the company of Christ, in His glory, and to be at ease.

A Reflection on the Transfiguration

Jesus the Christ

To help place the transfiguration in context, it is worth remembering Christ's powerful, enduring command to His disciples, "A new command I give you: Love one another. As I have loved you, so you must love one another." (John 13:34). One implication of His command, which included the phrase "as I have loved you", is that He has already demonstrated to His disciples the nature, motivation, character and behaviour of love. So consistent, persistent, pure and untarnished has been His love to His disciples that He can, with no ambiguity and no hesitancy, command His disciples to love one another as He has loved them. Another implication is that Christ's actions in leading the three disciples up the mount and enabling them to experience His transfiguration is illustrative of His love for them. How might this be a loving act?

Firstly, it provided confirmation of His status, His standing, His authority and His mission. His status was being God's Son (Matthew 17:5; Mark 9:7; Luke 9:35). His standing was that He was beloved by God. His authority was such that He should be listened to — on the mount God told the disciples specifically that they should listen to His Son (Matthew 17:5). Hence, one key aspect of His mission, implicit to the authority given to Him, was that He should teach. In speaking directly to the three disciples, God gave them confidences that they could rely on; an assurance that Jesus Christ was God's Son, that God greatly loved Him, that He should be listened to and, by inference, He would instruct. However, these confidences obviously were not seared into the hearts and minds of these disciples, as their later behaviour reveals. Nevertheless, the event of the transfiguration, in which those confidences were partially embedded (key others being the crucifixion and resurrection), was a powerful memory for all these disciples.

Peter witnessed the transfiguration, resurrection and the Pentecostal blessing of the Holy Spirit. In addition, many scholars link him to the writing of the Gospel of Mark. Its first verse testifies that Jesus Christ is the Son of God: "The beginning of the gospel about Jesus Christ, the Son of God." (Mark 1:1). The writing of that verse is a confidence founded on many circumstances and events, including the transfiguration where Peter heard God say, "This is my Son, whom I love" (Mark 9:7).

Not only did God's audible words to Peter and the other disciples give them assurances about Jesus Christ, but also so did the earlier actions of Christ, and the later actions of Elijah and Moses. Days earlier, in the region of Caesarea Philippi, Christ had asked His disciples, "Who do people say the Son of Man is?" They replied how some said John the Baptist, others Elijah, others Jeremiah or one of the prophets. Then Christ asked, "But you, who do you say I am?" It was Peter who replied, "You are the Christ, the Son of the living God." (Matthew 16:13-16; Mark 8:27-29; Luke 9:18-20). Christ's response to Peter's answer was, "Blessed are you, Simon son of Jonah, for this was not revealed to you by man, but by my Father in heaven." (Matthew 16:17). So here, before the event of the transfiguration, Peter's view was that Jesus Christ was the "Son of the living God" and Christ, in His reply to Peter, confirmed that view. Christ's comment to Peter also revealed that Christ was aware that His Father was already active, generating a realisation in Peter that Jesus was the Christ (i.e. messiah or anointed one), the Son of the living God. The transfiguration was further confirmation. Then later, the resurrection was unique ratification.

Peter's view of the messianic Christ was formed during a period when there were other messianic claimants. After the failure of the Hasmonean Kingdom (37 BC), the populist Jewish view of the messiah was someone who would deliver the Jews from oppression and usher in an Olam Haba ("world to come") or messianic era. Examples of messianic claimants just before or during the life of Peter include Simon of Peraea (~ 4 BC) and Athronges (~ 4-2 BC) who both led separate uprisings against the Herodians and the Romans. They appear to have declared themselves kings and may have claimed messianic status. Other likely claimants were Judas the Galilean (6 AD) and Theudas (~ 46 AD), who also led uprisings against the Romans. Peter's view that Jesus was *the* messiah needed to be formed against the backdrop of competing claimants. Certainly, the transfiguration helped confirm the assessment that Jesus was the true messiah.

On the mountain, during the transfiguration, Peter, James and John saw and heard for themselves that Christ was *not* Elijah, and that He was *not* Moses. The disciples heard Jesus in conversation with Elijah and Moses, with their names almost certainly being used during the conversation. Therefore, the disciples would not have needed to impute or guess who was in conversation with Jesus. It is Peter who in recognition of Moses and Elijah being present, asks Christ: "If you approve, I will put up three tents here, one for you, one for Moses, and one for Elijah." (Matthew 17:4).

Before their eyes and ears, the disciples learned that Jesus was not Elijah and that He was not Moses. Moreover, such was the status of Christ that Moses and Elijah were talking to Him about what *He* was soon to do in Jerusalem. Christ was the person being respected by Moses and Elijah. He was the centre of their conversation. Moses was honoured by Jews throughout history as the lawgiver. Elijah was viewed as preeminent among the prophets. Yet here, these two giants in Jewish history are together in focused conversation with the Christ about His future actions.

When Peter, and the others, heard God say, "This is my Son, whom I love." (Mark 9:7), this was confirmation that not only was Christ not Elijah or Moses, as some others had suggested, but that Christ was God's Son. God's words confirmed what Christ had earlier said to Peter: "Blessed are you, Simon son of Jonah, for this was not revealed to you by man, but by *my Father* in heaven." (Matthew 16:17).

As a small diversion, it is worth highlighting that Moses led the Israelites out of Egypt yet was not allowed by God to enter the holy land (Deuteronomy 32:51–52) due to his disobedience. Moses died on a mountain from which he could see into Israel, the promised land; the land he was barred from entering. Yet later, here at the transfiguration, he stood on another mountain, this time within Israel, but more importantly, he stood near Christ. Here on this mountain, Christ's true nature was revealed, the glorified, radiant person; the person respected by Moses and Elijah, the focus of their attention; yet above all, beloved by God.

In the transfiguration, lovingly God also provides the disciples with yet another opportunity for them to learn more about Christ's death: His readiness to die, His foreknowledge of His death and His preparedness to discuss His death. The three disciples also witnessed Moses' and Elijah's acceptance of Christ's death. There was no remonstration or dissent from Moses and Elijah, in contrast to Peter's rejection firstly of Christ's need to die (Matthew 16:22) and his later rejection of even knowing Christ (Luke 22:54-58).

Interestingly, the transfiguration and Moses' interaction with God atop a mountain (Exodus 24 and 34) display some parallels (see Table 1).

Table 1: Parallels between Moses on Mt Sinai and
Jesus on the mount of transfiguration

Moses at Mt Sinai	Jesus on the mount of transfiguration
Moses goes with three named individuals (Aaron, Nadab and Abihu) plus seventy of the elders up the mountain (Exodus 24:1,9).	Jesus takes three named disciples (James, Peter and John) up the mountain (Mark 9:2).
Moses' skin shines when he descends from the mountain after talking with God (Exodus 34:29).	Jesus is transfigured and his clothes become radiantly white (Mark 9:2-3).
A cloud envelopes the mountain top (Exodus 24:15-16, 18).	A cloud envelopes the mountaintop and the disciples (Mark 9:7).
God speaks from the cloud (Exodus 24:16).	God speaks from the cloud (Mark 9:7).
People are filled with fear and wonder when Moses' face was radiant (Exodus 34:30,32).	The disciples are fearful during the transfiguration (Mark 9:6; Luke 9:34) and soon after it, people are filled with wonder over Christ (Mark 9:15).

What later became appreciated by the disciples was not only Christ's need and willingness to sacrificially die, but also that He had power over death (John 10:18). This power, most evidenced by His rising, was also on display when He commanded Lazarus to rise from the dead. Similarly He commanded Jairus's daughter back from the dead and on another occasion He raised the dead son of the widow from the village of Nain (Luke 7:11–17). Saint Paul, in the initial sentences of his letter to the faithful in Rome, comments that Christ "was declared with power to be the Son of God by his resurrection from the dead:" (Romans 1:4).

God is Light

Despite all the different descriptions of 'light' that characterise the gospels' reports of the transfiguration, the overriding lasting impression, consistent among all the accounts, is the presence of unusual, unique light. The brilliant, startling light is consistent with Jesus's status as the Light of the world and as the Morning Star (Revelation 22:16) that signals the imminent arrival of the full light of day. John who witnessed the transfiguration later writes in the letter we know as 1 John that "God is light; in Him there is no darkness at all." (1 John 1:5).

Light illuminates what is present. Light reveals. It exposes flaws, imperfections, shortcomings and weaknesses as well as showing all that is commendable, attractive, beautiful, useful and winsome. Light exposes, makes vulnerable, yet it also protects because it reveals the true situation. It enlarges trust because of the clarity, the enlarged vista and exposure of detail that light reveals. The clarity light provides generates a comfort, an assurance, a confidence, a trustworthiness.

During the transfiguration where the Light of God shone, it is interesting to contrast the demeanour and behaviour of Moses, Elijah and the disciples. Moses and Elijah were able to move, to listen and speak and engage with Christ with surety. They could bask in His Light, His glory. They were not disturbed or disquieted by Christ's glory. Unlike the disciples, they were familiar with His Light. It was His trustworthy presence. By contrast the disciples were seemingly incapacitated, frightened (Mark 9:6), able to see and hear but when they spoke, or at least when Peter spoke, it was panicked words propelled by fear, not comfort or ease.

The writer of Luke's gospel says of Peter's words, "He did not know what he was saying." (Luke 9:34).

For the disciples, Christ's Light was a fearsome novelty. The writer of Mark's gospel says of Peter "..he did not know what to answer; for they became terrified." (Mark 9:6, NASB). Other translations use similar words such as "sore afraid" (KJV), "frightened" (NIV) or in the Greek, literally "out of one's wits". So here, all three disciples were filled with terror and fear, and when Peter blurted out his keenness to erect shelters, so wrapped in fright was he, that he had no idea what he was actually saying. By contrast, the interaction with Christ by Moses and Elijah was empathetic, purposeful, engaging and lacking in terror. In short, Moses and Elijah were comfortable in the presence of the glorified Christ whereas the disciples were not.

Peter had seen the confident comfort of Moses and Elijah in the presence of Christ. Yet by contrast, Peter was panicked and babbled. Later, on reflection, he would know, for he had witnessed it, that it was possible to be in the company of Christ, in His glory, and to be at ease. On the mount, Peter was disquieted; Moses and Elijah were not.

The fear experienced by the disciples when exposed to God's glory was not unique. Decades earlier, the shepherds near Bethlehem were left terrified when one of God's angels appeared to them and the "glory of God shone around them." (Luke 2:9).

It was many years later when Peter, then an older man, would write "let your adorning be the hidden person of the heart with the imperishable beauty of a gentle and quiet spirit, which in God's sight is very precious." (1 Peter 3:4). Moses and Elijah were like Adam and Eve in Eden before the Fall. In Eden, there was ease and harmony. Fear, discomfort and terror were absent. Adam and Eve were sinless, at ease in the company of God with no compunction to hide. They had no reason to be ashamed or frightened. Similarly, at the transfiguration Elijah and Moses felt no shame. They were not cowered by the Light of Christ. They were at ease, confident to interact. By contrast, the disciples, marred by sin, in the presence of transfigured Christ were sore afraid, disquieted and panicked. It is Christ who needs to call to His prostrate disciples, "Get up, don't be afraid." (Matthew 17:7).

Sometimes fear is so powerful that our senses are impaired. We fail to hear all that is said. We act in seemingly irrational ways. Sometimes our memory seems to bury or blot out aspects of exceedingly painful, fearful events. Yet the disciples obviously did remember much of this fearful interaction with Christ. Even Peter, who succumbed to panicked babbling on the mountainside, later is able to write:

"For he received honour and glory from God the Father when the voice came to him from the Majestic Glory, saying, "This is my Son, whom I love; with him I am well pleased." We ourselves heard this voice that came from heaven when we were with him on the sacred mountain." (2 Peter 1:17-18)

For Peter the transfiguration was a powerful reality that stayed with him. Remembering the event was a source of confidence and comfort; not re-lived fear and unease.

A question for me was — What is the significance and purpose of the appearance of Moses and Elijah being in conversation with Christ at his transfiguration? One insight is that both are signs that resurrection is possible. Although Moses was known to have died and even though the archangel Michael disputed with Satan about the body of Moses (Jude 1:9), here is Moses alive, talking to the Christ. Similarly, Elijah who disappeared in a whirlwind, centuries earlier, is here alive in conversation with the Christ.

Another insight, personally valuable for me, is the demonstration to the disciples that it is and will be possible to be like Moses and Elijah, insofar as the disciples need not anticipate trembling or shuddering when they eventually will be with Christ in His glory. God's grace and His work of purification and glorification makes us fit to be in His presence and to have no shame in being in His presence. I find that a great solace. It is like a return to Eden where the interaction between God and Adam and Eve had no shame; it was unstrained.

However, the chief purpose of the transfiguration would seem to be to cement a confidence in the disciples that Jesus was the *Christ, God's Son*. He was not Elijah, nor Moses. Christ's love for these disciples was shown by Him building up in them a rich wealth of aural and visual memories, including the transfiguration, which the Spirit of God could draw upon to establish, in the disciples, confidences in Christ and a love for Him. These disciples saw Him raise the dead, heal the sick, give sight to the blind, heal the lame and free the possessed. They saw Him walk on water. They saw Him read and expound the scriptures. They heard Him teach. They walked and ate with Him. They saw Him in prayer, in death and in resurrection. They heard God say, "This is my Son, whom I love; with him I am well pleased." — Jesus the Christ; God's Son. These were the rich visual, aural and emotion-filled memories the disciples could readily feast upon and the Spirit of God could use to reveal Christ as God's Son.

God's Love

When the disciples are led to see Christ, in His startling glory and in the company of the biblical greats of the Old Testament, what did God wish the disciples to learn about this person we call Jesus Christ? Strikingly, what God wanted the disciples to most know about Jesus Christ was His status; "This is my Son" (Luke 9:35; Mark 9:7).

Just pause and imagine as a disciple you have just learned, via the voice of God that Jesus Christ is God's Son. By implication, you have just heard Christ's Father speaking. What next would you expect God the Father to say concerning His Son? The inadequate earthly analogy is of a father speaking about his son to his son's friends. What would we expect that father to say? Perhaps, most often we might expect statements about the son's successes; evidencing the pride of the father.

Boldly and plainly what God says to the disciples is that He loves His Son; "This is my Son, whom I love." (Mark 9:7). Although Christ is visually dazzling and in the company of some giants of the Old Testament, none of that grandeur is mentioned by God. What God wishes the disciples to learn about Himself, and His Son, is simply and hugely that God loves Him.

At core, what does a son or daughter most want to hear and experience from their father? Simply that they are truly, genuinely, wholesomely loved. In the case of God's love, such is its power, purity and pre-eminence that God immediately wanted the disciples to learn that His love was showered on His Son. It was not the previous or future achievements of Christ, nor His emblazoned glory that God wished to highlight to the disciples. Rather it was that Jesus Christ firstly was His Son and secondly that God loved Him.

In summary, the transfiguration enabled the disciples to learn firstly the status of Christ, as God's Son. Secondly, they learned about God's response to His Son. The Father loved the Son.

A Person's Glory

The scriptures contain descriptions of God and His interaction with a range of people down through the centuries. The scriptures also contain descriptions of people and their interaction with God and with one another. One of the descriptions of humanity in scripture is that people can have glory; they can be glorious.

As mentioned in a previous section, the main, most frequent Hebrew word translated as glory in the Old Testament is the Hebrew word kbd, transliterated into English as *kabowd* or *kavod* and more rarely *kabod*. Its root meaning is "heavy". The weightiness (i.e. heaviness) of a person was their status, wealth or position and this was their glory. A man's wealth and the pomp of his surroundings were called his *kabod*; his glory. Rich people were "heavy" with wealth. Even now, centuries later, a similar sentiment applies in common parlance when we say of a wealthy individual that "they are loaded"; and one of the remaining, little used, English dictionary meanings of glory is a state of greatest prosperity.

In the Old Testament, a person could be loaded or made glorious by virtue of their power, position, achievement, reputation or honour. Hence, illustrations of a person's glory include:

(i)   Joseph's glory (Genesis 45:13) by virtue of his position in Egypt,
(ii) Samuel's glory (1 Samuel 9:6) was being highly respected as a man of God, as everything he said came true,
(iii) the glory of David (Psalm 21:5) and Jehoiakim (Jeremiah 22:18) was the stature of their royal positions in Judah,

(iv) Joshua's glory (Numbers 7:20) lay in his position of authority over the people of Israel,

(v) the glory of young men (Proverbs 20:29) was their strength,

(vi) the glory of the elderly (Proverbs 16:31) was their long life,

(vii) Jacob's glory (Genesis 30:43-31:1) lay in the multitude of his servants and animals.

A person's glory was the positive characteristic that underpinned their favourable renown or acclaim. For example, the wealth of possessions of a rich person's household was their glory. Such wealth, the foundation of their glory, could not, however, be carried by that person beyond death (Psalm 49:17). Psalm 39:6 bluntly reminds us:

> "Man is a mere phantom as he goes to and fro:
> He bustles about, but only in vain;
> he heaps up wealth, not knowing who will get it."

There is an old proverb starkly reminding all of the limitations imposed by death —'Shrouds have no pockets'. Wealth that serves people in their earthly realm cannot be pocketed to serve them subsequently. Human perishability is described further in Psalm 49:12-13:

> "But man, despite his riches, does not endure;
> He is like the beasts that perish.
> This is the fate of those who trust in themselves,
> and of their followers, who approve their sayings."

In his general epistle, Peter reminds his readers:

> "All men are like grass,
> And all their glory is like the flowers of the field;
> The grass withers and the flowers fall,
> But the word of the Lord stands for ever." (1 Peter 1:24-25)

A person's earthly power and position ends with their death, and often sooner. Their achievements, reputation or honour can live on in the minds and hearts of those who remember them. Their financial wealth passes out of their hands onto others. Some live on in the pages and documents of history. However, for most people, their earthly glory rapidly fades. History teaches us that history remembers and honours only a tiny fraction of all who have lived on the earth.

Death may not be the only point in time after which a person's glory will likely fade. Proverbs 20:29 states the glory of young men is their strength. Yet we all know that the relentless process of ageing eventually robs us of strength, agility, endurance, speed and finesse. We fade away. Saint Paul, in one of his letters to the Corinthians, notes this about himself and his colleagues "… outwardly we are wasting away," (2 Corinthians 4:16). Accident, acts of violence, disease and misfortune can arrive at our door at any age and lessen or remove those things that are the foundation of our earthly glory, our acclaim and favourable reputation. Therefore, our earthly glory may not solely end or fade with our death.

At the dawn of time, as noted in scripture, people were made in God's likeness (Genesis 1:26-27) with God-given dignity and authority. This was their glory. God had blessed humanity. They were given power and responsibility to be rulers of their environment, to be recipients of seed-bearing plants and harvesters of bountiful fruit trees. So productive was Nature that there was no environmental stress. In the largess and safety of those surroundings people were encouraged to become parents (Genesis 1:28-29). In Eden, humanity had a glory —a dignity, authority, a grandness and euphony. However, this glory became tainted, lessened and marred by sin (Genesis3: 16-19). The mark or stain of sin caused humanity to fall short of the glory God gave and intended for all people (Romans 3:23). The purity of care for one another became sullied. Accusation and blaming commenced. Envy and violence were unleashed, and shortly led to murder (Genesis 4:8). Enjoyment and respect for the beauty of the human form became subject to abuse, immorality and adultery (Deuteronomy 22:25-27; Leviticus 18:7; Leviticus 18:10; Leviticus 18:20).

Woman is the glory of man

Any study of scriptural references to a person's glory is likely to come across an intriguing statement from Saint Paul about the glory of a man

27

and a woman. Paul's statement, at face value, is interesting because it implies that not only can a person have earthly glory but that a man can be the "glory of God". In 1 Corinthians 11:7, specifically of males, Paul writes, "he is the image and glory of God". Then immediately he adds that; "the woman is the glory of man." Now, in my view and in the views of many commentators, this is one example of where quoting a single verse in abstraction from its surrounding text and textual setting is fraught with danger. Yet, unfortunately many preachers and teachers have done so, quoting this verse in abstraction and using Paul's comments to make claims and imputations about men and women that are misguided or plainly wrong; or which support particular cultural mores.

So, starting with Paul's first comment that a man "is the image and glory of God", what does he mean? Firstly, regarding the phrase describing how a man "is the image of God" reminds his audience that humans, like all of creation, were at their outset qualitatively "very good" (Genesis 1:31). In their persons was a nature resonant with God's image such that people could be patient, compassionate, faithful, truthful, trustworthy, kind, and just; reflective of God's image.

But what of the phrase that <u>man</u> "is the glory of God"? Before providing an answer to that question, it is worth stating at the outset that many commentators openly acknowledge that this particular section (1 Corinthians 11:2-16) in which Paul's particular comment resides is a difficult passage to comprehend. Verlyn Verbrugge who wrote the commentary notes on 1 Corinthians in the Expositor's Bible Commentary: Revised Edition (2008) plainly says, "This section is, beyond any doubt, one of the most difficult to understand in 1 Corinthians and, indeed, in the Bible as a whole. There are almost as many interpretations of this passage as there are interpreters,.." (p. 350).

I leave it to interested readers to examine for themselves the many alternative interpretations of the key material in 1 Corinthians 11:2-16. Suffice to say that in my view when we read the statement that man is "the glory of God" it is important to remember that the word Paul uses here, translated as glory, is the Greek word doxa.

In the New Testament the word doxa does often mean glory; but it does not solely and always mean glory. In fact, in the New Testament, the following frequencies of words for doxa apply: glory (n=145), glorious (n=10), honour (n=6), praise (n=4), dignity (n=2) and worship (n=1). Moreover, as previously mentioned, the statement by the nineteenth century commentator Albert Barnes is worth noting; "when the classic writers used the word 'glory' they were referring to (i) opinion, sentiment or (ii) fame, reputation or (iii) splendour and brightness."

Thus, when Paul indicates that a man is "the *doxa* of God"; several interpretations are feasible. Of the many possibilities, those that make most sense, at least to me, are those that stress that man is the doxa (the honouring) of God. Having or creating honour is one of the meanings of glory and, in this particular case; it seems to me apt to draw on the concept of honour or honouring. Man's purpose is to honour God. The Westminster Catechism's first question and answer is:

Q: What is the chief end of man?

A: Man's chief end is to glorify God, and to enjoy him forever.

We exist to praise and honour God, by living in relationship to God, we reflect His glory and so in that sense are His glory. To say we are the doxa (the honour or honouring) of God is another way of saying the first commandment. Remember the conversation in which a Pharisee who was a noted expert in the Law purposefully tested Christ by asking Him: "Teacher, which is the greatest commandment in the Law?" Jesus replied: "Love the Lord your God with all your heart and with all your soul and with all your mind." This is the first and greatest commandment." (Matthew 22:36-38).

To love God is to *honour*, respect, cherish and serve Him. At the core of a person, their chief purpose is to be honouring of God; to be full of love for Him and devoted to Him. In stating this commandment, Christ makes no distinction between men and women. All should be honouring of God and in that sense reflect His honour.

So why does Paul then go on to say that women (and not men) are the "glory of man"? Firstly, it is important to note that in this passage when Paul mentions women he does so in the context of marriage and in the context of Corinthian society and the accepted role of women in that particular society in that era. Corinth in Paul's era was a collectivist society. This meant that social conformity and the greater good of society was considered far more important than an individual's rights or happiness. In addition, this collectivist society had the underpinning of an honour-shame paradigm whereby a person's behaviour was judged as bringing honour or shame to their family. Hence, an acknowledged important role for a wife in a household in that society was to act in ways that served and protected the reputation and honour of her entire family, which included honouring her husband. In such a society, family members, especially women, who displayed aberrant behaviour or loose morals, risked bringing dishonour on their entire family, but especially on the family's senior male. Hence, in this social context not only was it important for a woman to honour God but in addition, in that society, she needed to behave in ways that brought honour to her husband and therefore the wider family. This stress by Paul on the need to be honouring would have seemed reasonable and appropriate, given the nature of the honour-shame culture of Corinth at that time.

Even nowadays, the need for a wife to be honouring of her husband continues to be reflected in many marriage vows. However, the difference between modern times and cultural mores in Paul's era is that the admonition to love and honour now applies equally to men and women. By illustration, when couples wed in the Roman Catholic Church the marriage vows, according to the rite of marriage, have this customary text: *I, _____, take you, _____, to be my (husband/wife). I promise to be true to you in good times and in bad, in sickness and in health. I will love you and honour you all the days of my life.*

Paul's observation that a person at best honours God or is "the honouring" of God can be complemented by a somewhat similar observation of Peter. Peter notes, "..your genuine faith, which is more valuable than gold that perishes when tested by fire, may result in praise, glory, and honor when Jesus, the Messiah, is revealed." (1 Peter 1:7, ISV). Faith is the honouring of God; a genuine devotion to Him. When Peter speaks of "genuine faith", resulting "in praise, glory, and honor when Jesus, the Messiah, is revealed"; another way of saying this is that genuine honouring of God can generate praise, glory, and honour when Jesus returns. Hence, if asked, "Is there anything of our days on the earth that is generative of the glory of heaven rather than the inescapable fading away of our earthly glory?" — the answer is yes! Generative of heavenly glory, praise and honour is our genuine honouring of Him. Our devotion to Christ, our love for Him and obedience to Him creates the reciprocity of praise, glory, and honour to and in Him when He returns but also while we live on earth.

Paul makes this last point in 2 Corinthians 3:18; "And we, who with unveiled faces all reflect the Lord's glory, are being transformed into his likeness with ever-increasing glory, which comes from the Lord, who is the Spirit." The "increasing glory" which Paul mentions "comes from the Lord". It is His glory not our personal glory which increases and it is the reflected glory of God. The reflected display of His glory in us is via our being transformed into His likeness.

This transformation is a work of the Spirit of God. God's Spirit creates in us an appetite and willingness to know and serve God. It is God's Spirit who produces in us "love, joy, peace, patience, kindness, goodness, faithfulness, gentleness and self-control." (Galatians 5:22). Our attitudes and behaviours are able to change due to the work of God's Spirit. When we act as His servant, His son or daughter, then His brightness and rightness is reflected out into the world around us.

Faith, the honouring of God, plays an important role in being generative of this "increasing glory" and the glory of heaven. First, however, comes grace. God's grace is poured out for all people through the death of His one and only Son, Jesus. Then it is by God's grace, through the exercising of God's gift of faith (honouring, devotion and trust in Him), that we are saved and empowered by His Spirit. All people receive God's grace, all are given a measure of faith by God (Romans 12:3), all are enabled, made able, to exercise that faith, the honouring of Him, should they choose so. Hence, Paul is able to say, "For by such grace you have been saved through faith. This does not come from you; it is the gift of God." (Ephesians 2:8).

Grace is God's unmerited favour — something done for us without our help and is undeserved. Faith is each person's positive response to God, a decision to believe, trust and honour that comes from being enabled by God freely to choose Him. In choosing Him and receiving God's gift of His Spirit that same Spirit enables us to act in ways that allow the reflection of God's glory, His majesty and authority.

Glory outside the Scriptures

Aside from its use in the scriptures, the word glory is mentioned in important Christian creedal statements like the Nicene Creed that states:

> He will come again in *glory*
> to judge the living and the dead
> and his kingdom will have no end.
> ......
> I believe in the Holy Spirit, the Lord, the giver of life,
> who proceeds from the Father and the Son,
> who with the Father and the Son is adored and *glorified*,......

A common ending of the Lord's Prayer features the word glory:

> For thine is the kingdom,
> The power, and the *glory*,
> For ever and ever. Amen.

The word glory often features in hymns of praise. One example is the popular hymn "To God be the Glory" written by Fanny Crosby (1875).

> To God be the *glory*, great things He hath done,
> So loved He the world that He gave us His Son,
> Who yielded His life an atonement for sin,
> And opened the life gate that all may go in.

As an aside, Fanny was blind almost from birth yet she wrote over 4,000 songs and hymns and used over 200 nom de plumes. She had a prodigious memory, committing to heart by the age of ten, the first four books of the Old Testament and all four gospels.

In England, a perennially favourite hymn is "Land of Hope and Glory". Its popular chorus begins as follows:

> Land of Hope and *Glory*, Mother of the Free,
> How shall we extol thee, who are born of thee?

Glory is a word not restricted to Christendom and its sacred writings, nor is it a word confined to the annals of history. It has remained in frequent and persistent use in the English language. The word glory has continued to be used down through the centuries to our current era. In our age it is not unusual to hear people talking about 'glorious sunshine' on a warm, fine day; or their favourite team having a 'glorious win' or someone having a 'glorious time' or describing a colleague as 'glorying in their success'.

To this day, theatres still celebrate Shakespearean plays, like Henry VIII, which contain memorable statements about glory. In Henry VIII, act 3, sc.2, l.224-6 Wosley comments on the eventual fading of his human glory by saying:

> "I have touch'd the highest point of all my greatness,
> And from that full meridian of my glory I haste now to my setting."

Reflections on Glory
in the Scriptures

The Lure of Earthly Glory

The Old Testament's use of the word glory, as attached to a person, conveys the weight or importance of that person's status, wealth, acclaim, ability or position. Yet the Old Testament also teaches that this glory mostly fades. The strength and energy of a person's youth gives way to the frailty of their old age. Youthful beauty dwindles to be replaced by the blemished diminished stature of the elderly. What wealth we have passes to others.

Human glory is mostly evanescent. In the end, the vast majority of us disappear, largely unnoticed, into the annals of human history. Even in a single lifetime, one's human glory can come and go; appear, disappear and re-appear, but usually in old age, it mostly fades. As previously quoted, Paul, in one of his letters to the Corinthians, notes the same about himself and his colleagues "… outwardly we are wasting away," (2 Corinthians 4:16). Although eventually our human glory wanes, it can also end abruptly, at any age. Accident, misfortune, disease, malevolence and strife can lessen or remove our earthly glory.

Yet human glory is magnetic for many. Like moths to a light, we find earth-bound glory ever so attractive. Its absence can be a source of shame, envy or depression. Most of us invest time, energy, talents and money in some sort of quest for this glory of wealth, ability, status, respect, longevity, influence, bodily beauty or power. The quest for glory can be deeply earnest and all-consuming or by contrast, it can be a tepid, weak, almost inconsequential endeavour. Often the glory of wealth, ability, status, respect, longevity, bodily beauty or power arises from circumstance, genetic heritage, culture, familial expectations or a person's natural or developed abilities and ambitions. It can also accompany a person's walk with God.

The gaining of glory need not be inherently wrong, misleading or deserving of shame or misgiving. Remember Psalm 139:14 that says, "I praise you, for I am fearfully and wonderfully made." A person's skill, natural beauty, magnetism, depth of insight, carefulness and ability to empathise can be a demonstration of how wonderfully they are made. In his letter to Timothy, Paul reminds him (and us) that "..everything created by God is good and nothing is to be rejected." (1 Timothy 4:4). Paul also encourages the giving of thanks; "I urge, then, first of all, that requests, prayers, intercession and *thanksgiving* be made for everyone." (1 Timothy 2:1).

Therefore, it is sad that one risk surrounding human glory is that some people wrongly avoid being thankful, not only regarding others, but also especially concerning the wonder of themselves. Either they do not perceive that there is anything wonderful or special about themselves and so express shame or disappointment over themselves. Or else, they become ashamed or embarrassed by their natural prowess or favoured circumstance. Seeing themselves as inferior, or wishing to avoid being seen as superior, can lead some people to thinking that the exercise of legitimate ambition or natural talent is inherently wrong. Yet, avoiding sloth, slovenliness and ineptitude that arise from laziness deserves congratulation. Paul writes to Timothy about the reasonable reward for hard work: "It is the hard-working farmer who ought to have the first share of the crops." (2 Timothy 2:6).

Enjoying the beauty of the human form, the physical, mental and creative talents of people is to glimpse how we are "fearfully and wonderfully made" (Psalm 139:14) and this should be a cause to thank God for the wonder of His creation. Moreover, remember the words of Paul that "*thanksgiving* be made for everyone" (1 Timothy 2:1), not just those coated with the glory of skill, power, natural beauty, energy or wealth.

Using one's talents, circumstance and ambition for the sake of one's family or for the sake of others can be commendable. However, the achievement of human glory is not without risk. A danger in seeking or achieving human glory is when it becomes a false god, when it becomes an end in itself, worshipped and sought after for its own sake rather than serving Him.

There is a risk that we live to serve only or mostly those who can enlarge our earthly glory, rather than being attuned to serving and honouring "Our Father" (Matthew 6:9-10). The apostle Paul was ever alert to this danger, writing to the Philippians that they should "Do nothing out of selfish ambition or vain conceit." (Philippians 2:3). Centuries earlier, a psalmist wrote:

"In prosperity people lose their good sense,
they become no better than dumb animals.
So they go on in their self-assurance,
right up to the end they are content with their lot." (Psalm 49: 12-13, Jerusalem Version).

In this same Psalm is the caution:

"Do not be overawed when someone gets rich, and lives in ever greater splendour;
when he dies he will take nothing with him, his wealth will not go down with him.
Though he pampered himself while he lived -- and people praise you for looking after yourself--he will go to join the ranks of his ancestors, who will never again see the light."
(Psalm 49: 16-19, Jerusalem Version).

It is easy to understate the lure of human glory as a false god, so attractive and captivating is its spell and so skilful are we at rationalising our actions. It is especially worth noting that one of the temptations of Christ, in fact the last temptation Satan placed before Him, was the lure of earthly glory. Matthew 4:8-9 records:

"Again, the devil took him to a very high mountain and showed him all the kingdoms of the world and their *glory*.

> And he said to him, "All these I will give you, if you will
> fall down and worship me.""

Christ was offered the splendour and riches of the nations. Their glory was a prize and reward for worshipping Satan. However, this lure of earthly glory (wealth, grandeur and status), as the reward for worshipping Satan, was rebuffed by Christ. Rather, Christ reminded Satan of the preeminent requirement to worship the Lord God and to serve Him. Matthew 4:10 outlines Christ's response where He remembered and repeated God's words. Matthew 4:11 then describes the aftermath of the temptation.

> "Then Jesus said to him, "Be gone, Satan! For it is written,
> "'You shall worship the Lord your God and him only shall
> you serve.'"
> Then the devil left him, and behold, angels came and were
> ministering to him." (Matthew 4:10-11)

It is worth noting that Christ's defence against acquiring earthly treasures, conditional on His worship of Satan, was Christ's remembrance of the words God gave to be written down. Deuteronomy 6:13 says, "Thou shalt fear the LORD thy God, and serve him, and shalt swear by his name." and Deuteronomy 10:20 says, "Thou shalt fear the LORD thy God; him shalt thou serve, and to him shalt thou cleave, and swear by his name." Hence, a lesson for us each is that a bulwark against the lure of earthly glory that can lead us away from God, is remembrance of His words, the scriptures passed down to us from the ancient of days. In addition, not only are the scriptures a lamp for our feet and a light for our path (Psalm 119:105) but He additionally has given us a Counsellor and Teacher; His Spirit. The apostle John, for example, is enabled to remember that Christ said, "..the Counsellor, the Holy Spirit, whom the Father will send in my name, will teach you all things and will remind you of everything I have said to you." (John 14:26). In short, John was enabled to remember that he would be enabled to remember what Christ said!

In contrast to Christ who only served the will of His Father; we are marred by sin. Despite giving us His words that can aid and protect us, and despite the gift of the Counsellor and Teacher, our service is not always to God. We are led astray, at times too easily diverted. We do something or nothing, but not the wholly right thing. We have human eyes that find earth-bound human glory attractive. Often earth-bound riches, physical beauty, power and talent impress us. Yet, wonderfully made though we are — and we should thank God for our individual wonder — "The Lord does not look at the things man looks at. Man looks at the outward appearance, but the Lord looks at the heart." (1 Samuel 16:7).

The outward is so often the main basis for our assessment and judgment. A disfigured person can suffer further, by being shunned and avoided; solely due to the unattractiveness of their disfigurement. By contrast, a beautiful or handsome face can be sufficient rationale for initiation of wanted or unwanted conversation. Remember what Isaiah wrote of the Servant, "He had no beauty or majesty to attract us to him, nothing in his appearance that we should desire him." (Isaiah 53:2b). The implication is that Christ, the Servant, purposefully had no physical character or majesty to be visually magnetic. His outward appearance did not draw the crowds to Him.

In Eden before trust in God was withdrawn, there was euphony. There was no guesswork, reasoning or imputation required to counter cunning, malice or pride or give allowance for shame, embarrassment and inadequacy. The outer personage purely reflected the inner person. The transparent trustworthiness of humanity was seamlessly immersed in the beauty of creation. "God saw all that He had made, and it was very good." (Genesis 1:31). There was no degrading ageing, no arduous toiling, no barbs and thorns to bar progress and harm or scar bodies, no deceit to discern, no cunning to counter.

After Eden, we retained much of what was a mirror to its former perfection. The beauty of youth continued, before age and decay wearied all. The glory of youthfulness remained attractive. Even some angels wrongly were captivated by young women, and, in perversion, married them. "When men began to increase in number on the earth and daughters were born to them, the sons of God[2] saw that the daughters of men were beautiful, and they married any of them they chose." (Genesis 6:1,2).

Captivating though our glory can be, even to angels, and whilst it need not need be a source of shame or embarrassment insofar as our physical glory can be a reflection of our goodly beginnings in Eden, our glory nonetheless is NOT the means for being accepted by God. Although as part of His creation humanity was "very good" (Genesis 1:31), and we continue to be "fearfully and wonderfully made" (Psalm 139:14), and we should not be embarrassed by the beauty of the human form and our natural abilities, our acceptance by God is NOT due to the glory or the "goodness" of our creation.

What God finds acceptable, what He always welcomes and never scorns is truly felt awareness of the need of His love. There are many verses in scripture that convey that fact and sentiment.

> "My sacrifice, O God, is a broken spirit; a broken and contrite heart you, God, will not despise" (Psalm 51:17)

> "Blessed are the poor in spirit, for to them belongs the Kingdom of heaven." (Matthew 5:3)

> "A bruised reed he will not break, and a smouldering wick he will not snuff out." (Isaiah 42: 3)

> "..you have comforted me. Surely God is my salvation; I will trust and not be afraid. The LORD, the LORD, is my strength and my song; he has become my salvation." (Isaiah 12:1b-2)

> "O LORD Almighty, blessed is the man who trusts in you." (Psalm 84:12)

---

[2] The "sons of God" (Genesis 6:2, 4) is a phrase used three other times in the Bible outside of Genesis 6—Job 1:6; 2:1; 38:7. All these instances indicate the "sons of God" are spirit/angelic beings, suggesting that Genesis 6 is similarly speaking of spirits/angels.

"He will be the sure foundation for your times, a rich store of salvation and wisdom and knowledge; the fear of the LORD is the key to this treasure." (Isaiah 33:6)

"Righteousness [standing acceptable to God] will be granted and credited to us also who believe in [trust in, adhere to, and rely on] God, who raised Jesus our Lord from the dead," (Romans 4:24, Amplified Bible)

"For with the heart a person believes (adheres to, trusts in, and relies on Christ) and so is justified (declared righteous, acceptable to God), and with the mouth he confesses (declares openly and speaks out freely his faith) and confirms [his] salvation." (Romans 10:10, Amplified Bible)

It is important to highlight that the prayer that Jesus taught His disciples, in response to their request to be taught how to pray, begins with the words "Our Father". Christ was reminding His disciples that they stood in a legal relationship to God where God was their Father. One of many implications of God being our Father is that *our need* is to receive His care, protection, provision, guidance, support and love; for that is what God, the perfect Father, graciously gives to His children.

Additionally some wonderful verses in Isaiah summarise the need to rely on God. "Let him who walks in the dark, who has no light, trust in the name of the LORD and rely on his God." (Isaiah 50:10b). This same verse, however, is followed by another that is exposing, sobering and troubling because it describes those who fail to lean on God, but who instead rely *solely* on their own resources, skills, insights and knowledge.

"all you who light fires and provide yourselves with flaming torches,
go, walk in the light of your fires and of the torches you have set ablaze.
This is what you shall receive from my hand:
You will lie down in torment." (Isaiah 50:11).

Many of those who "walk in the light of your fires" would be rightly judged as people who are hardworking, diligent, strong, resourceful, and keen to reason a way forward. Nonetheless, by not placing any reliance in God or credence in Him, but rather solely relying on their own skill and reasoning (and those around them), in the end these same resourceful people find no enduring peace and no lasting comfort inasmuch as they have ignored the Comforter. This is not to criticise reasoning, logic and intellectual cleverness for they are what make some people "fearfully and wonderfully made" (Psalm 139:14). These characteristics can be part of a person's glory and can be used by God to draw people near to Him. However, if these characteristics are the *only* foundations of a person's life on earth, rather than choosing a reliance on God and His word, then sadly these people inevitably face God's judgement and not His acceptance.

A common societal illustration of the lure of earthly glory, souring into false worship, concerns using one's own human glory (fame, ability, wealth) to aid one's family or others. Reasoned behaviour, even faithful action, where the initial motivation generates care for one's family, or others, can become tainted and can turn perversely into self-serving acts whereby one's fame is promoted rather than the well-being of one's family or others or adhering to remaining faithful. The display of natural or developed talents that assists others can corrode into selfishness or self-centredness that seeks personal glory alone, often at the expense of some others. One's family or colleagues can end up being sacrificed, actively or passively, on the altar of the quest for success. Actions, once legitimate, can degrade into either self-serving ambition or a blind observance of the worldly mould of their era.

Thus, in summary, a natural prowess or one's fortunate circumstance can lead to behaviours whose motivation can be commendable or questionable. Actions and attitudes can sour into being mostly self-serving or without thoughtfulness or godly devotion. Put simply, one's human glory can be used for good or ill. It can arise from any point on a wide spectrum of motivations. It can be a by-product of a life attuned to the leadings of the Spirit of God. At worst, it can arise from a self-serving, manipulative endeavour, destructive of relationships and even the person's own earthly life.

Sometimes the ill is the lack of motivation; not even bothering to exercise one's talents or circumstance and thereby serving neither God nor one's neighbour. To that end, it is worth noting the parable of the talents (Matthew 25:14-30) where the servant who buried his talent (i.e. money) was judged by his master to be "bad and slothful". Although the servant did not steal or use the talent (i.e. money) for personal greed, and in that sense did no obvious wrong, he nonetheless due to his indolence achieved less than was easily possible, such as depositing the talent (i.e. money) to earn interest. In a similar vein, Albert Barnes points out, "God will judge people not merely for doing wrong, but for not "doing" right."

Perhaps a poignant illustration is King David's behaviour just prior to his adultery with Bathsheba, where in 2 Samuel 11:1 is the statement, "In the spring, at the time when kings go off to war, ... David remained in Jerusalem." His regal duty was to lead and be present with his troops but instead he tarried in Jerusalem. His behaviour in opting to remain in Jerusalem may not seem to be obviously wrong but it was the entre to great error and revealed his failure in that moment to wear the mantle of kingship God had placed on him (1 Samuel 16:13). The expression "from little things big things grow" applies in either direction, generating good or ill. For David the small act of indolent tarrying provided an opportunity that triggered adultery and then later David orchestrated an awful murder.

In short, earthly glory can have several causes and motivations, not all are worthy; but neither should all be criticised. It is reasonable to be rewarded for hard work and not to be lazy so that those that fall under one's care, either within one's family or in the workplace, receive sustenance, respect and wealth. Yet even these actions can become corrupted, ending with glory (acclaim, wealth, respect, power) being sought for its own sake. Seemingly being assiduous can actually lead one away from God and time in His company. Rather than serving and honouring one's family, community or workplace, with acclaim being the rightful outcome or the ramification of the prowess, diligence and activity, the thirst for acclaim becomes the main motivation, the underlying appetite. There is also the opposite or different situation where reasonable ambition is corrupted or eroded by laziness or paralysing fear. In this case, glory that could or should be the reward for endeavour is not received, due to inaction or an inability to act.

There are many examples in scripture of the corrupting thirst for human glory. One example is the disciples' repetitious appetite for status. The verses Mark 9:34, Luke 9:46, Mark 10:41 and Luke 22:24 all outline dispute and argument among the disciples about who among them was the greatest. The glory of status was a recurring enticement for the disciples during Christ's ministry. What must have been especially saddening for Christ was where and when those arguments over status arose. The first occasion was on the road to Capernaum, shortly after the spiritual intimacy of the transfiguration and the healing by Christ of the young boy possessed by an evil spirit. A second occasion was on the road to Jerusalem when the two brothers, James and John, privately asked Jesus if they could sit either side of the glorified Christ. When the other ten disciples heard about James and John's secret quest for preference, they were indignant. The third occasion was in Jerusalem at the supper Christ knew to be His last before His death. There the topic of who was the greatest among them arose again.

The verses in Mark 9: 33-34 and Luke 9:46 outline that the disciples were not engaged in amiable discussion, but rather that they disputed over who was or should be the greatest among them. It was a tangle of words with knife-edges. Peter, James and John, even after experiencing the intimacy of the transfiguration, were not immune from intense argument and rivalry over their status in the group of disciples. Even on the road to Jerusalem, their last long walk together, James and John privately approached Christ seeking the pre-eminent seats in heaven that would signal their greatness. Then later, on the solemn occasion of the Passover supper, with Christ loved by the Father yet soon to bear His wrath against Sin, all the disciples entered into interaction that again degenerated into dispute over who among them was the greatest. An appetite for food was not the only appetite on display at the Last Supper. Disconcertingly, the disciples' appetites extended to seeking fame among men, not solely fame with God.

On the first occasion of their disputation, Christ's response to their vying for supremacy was to wait until the group was together inside the house in Capernaum and there to ask them what they were arguing about while on the road. Their response was silence. Perhaps they were already ashamed of their behaviour. Christ then sits and calls them. His seated posture was the culturally known behaviour of a teacher. His message to them was powerful and seemingly simple: "If anyone wants to be first, he must be the very last, and the servant of all." (Mark 9:35).

Earthly glory as expressed by status and pre-eminence would dictate that first is best. The head, the chief, the master or leader is the culturally preferred position of dominance and oversight. Yet Christ says the first is the servant of all; not the master. Later at the Last Supper He says similar things in response to their repeated dispute over which of them was the greatest. He reminded them that He is the servant: "I am among you as one who serves." (Luke 22: 27). In His eyes, there was no glory in standing on or standing over others to seek pre-eminence. God called Christ not only "my Son, whom I love" (Mark 9:7) but also "my *servant*, whom I uphold" (Isaiah 42:1). In answering Satan's temptation, Christ quotes the scriptures "Worship the Lord your God, and *serve* him only." (Deuteronomy 10:20; Deuteronomy 6:13).

The disciples had forgotten the centrality of servitude. They had forgotten the insight and wisdom of David who in his psalm, we call Psalm 23, conveys the image of God as a servant. It is God, the servant, who prepares the table for David, so lavish and abundant that David's cup overflows and he comes to the realisation and assurance that "Surely goodness and love will follow me all the days of my life" (Psalm 23:6).

Christ, the servant (Isaiah 49:5; Luke 22:27), would have been saddened and wearied by observing that His disciples actively sought and competed for the status of perceived 'top dog'. Their jockeying for positions of pre-eminence showed that servitude was far from their thinking. Instead, they wanted to be or to know who was chief among them. Their motivation and underlying appetite was to achieve the glory of status, visible honour and observed social superiority.

So entrenched was this thirst for renown among these men that even three years in the company of the Lord Jesus Christ appeared not to diminish this inner drive for acclaim and culturally accepted status. Yet with God all things are possible. The Spirit of God is an effectual teacher. Hence, we read of eventual attitudinal and behavioural change in Peter, James and John. Explaining more, in the very first verse of the letter we call 1 Peter, Peter writes: "Simon Peter, a *servant* and apostle of Jesus Christ" (2 Peter 1:1). Similarly, in the very first verse of James' letter we read his words: "James, a *servant* of God and of the Lord Jesus Christ," (James 1:1).

Lastly, in the first verse of the book of Revelation we read of John named as Christ's *servant*.

The keenness of Peter, James and John to state at the outset of an interaction with their readers or listeners that they were *servants* of Christ is a long way from Peter, James and John arguing about which of them was the greatest in order to achieve the glory or acclaim of status.

Similarly, when Paul writes to the Romans, he begins his letter with the words, "Paul, a *servant* of Christ Jesus," (Romans 1:1) and elsewhere in his letters, he encourages his readers to "submit to one another out of reverence for Christ" and that "in humility consider others better than yourselves" (Philippians 2:3). These are the words of service and care, not words of domination, prestige and high rank.

In a similar vein, when reflecting on the glory of beauty, the apostle Peter makes the admonition; "Your beauty should not come from outward adornment….Instead, it should be that of your inner self, the unfading beauty of a gentle and quiet spirit, which is of great worth in God's sight." (1 Peter 3:3-4). It is not the perfection of a person's visage nor, as pointed out by Peter, the splendour of their garments that God sees and values. Rather, what is valued by God is a person's inner beauty, their gentleness and calm focus that finds its source in Him.

The captivation of earthly glory was not confined to the disciples. We still see it in our own age in the behaviour of some parents, starved of their own glory, yet seeking reflected glory through their children's success. Unfortunately, to achieve that glory, some of these parents make their love and respect for their children conditional on their children achieving success. Often these children will strive for success in order to gain the approval and love of their parents. However, if the children fail to match the expectations of their parents then the children are liable to wear the taint of being loved conditionally and feelings of inadequacy will gnaw away at their self-worth. Some of these children will grow to have a shame of themselves, as they have not achieved parental expectations. These children will brand themselves with failure. Devoid of praise and fame, which accompanies success, they will count themselves as inglorious. They may lash out in anger and frustration. They may curl up, shrivel and succumb to despair, devoid of the growth and protection that true affection affords.

Because these parents set the requirement of glory (i.e. success) as a condition of their respect and love, their corrupted affection for their children is utterly unlike the true love of God. God unconditionally loves. God loves us not because we achieve glory, not because we are beautiful, or skilful, or knowledgeable, or brilliant. The love God bestows on us is completely unmerited and undeserved. It is His grace.

Children who are unloved or only conditionally loved by their parents can find it difficult to sense or trust how they are greatly loved by God. These people can grow up in a household where parental love and care is either absent due to parents being overly busy and absent or where parental affection is constantly conditional on an unrealistic achievement of glory. Some children too often receive criticism, abuse and denigration rather than fair-minded discipline. These abused children find it difficult to empathise with David's declaration in Psalm 139:14 that says, "I praise you, for I am fearfully and wonderfully made." The damage to their self-worth, attributable to the corrosive, belittling or neglectful environment of their childhood, leads them to not easily trust how much, and how unconditionally, God loves them. They are special to Him, yet they find it difficult to believe this could be so. Loving our children, as Christ already does, as unconditionally as possible, makes it easier for our children to comprehend God's love for them. Comprehending the embrace of His love can facilitate our children's genuine, deep and consistent love for others. God's love for us does not depend on our earthly glory; neither should our love for our neighbour, especially where that neighbour is our child.

I repeat a story I heard some decades ago from Hans Bürki (1925-2002), a Swiss theologian and educational psychologist. He relayed an experiment conducted by a German psychologist that involved placing two chairs, facing one another, in a room with the psychologist seated on one of the chairs. He then invited, one at a time, small children to enter the room and sit on the other chair. As each child walked in, he would ask the child, "You are you a precious child. Are you not?"

He received from the children three main categories of response. One response was for the child to say strongly; "No, I'm not a precious child!" Their answer was often clipped, loud and definite. A second response was for the child to register disbelief; "Are you sure? Really? I don't know...

maybe?" In these cases, the child was unsure, not confident and full of doubt. The third response was often simply; "Yes, yes I'm a precious child!" Unsurprisingly, the explanation for these three different responses lay in the nature of the parenting the children had received.

Children displaying this last response came from families in which the parental affection for their children was warm, consistent, frequent and genuine. The parental care enlivened and secured these children. However, children displaying the first response came from households in which they received little affection. Some such children grow into adulthood, finding it hard to trust and acknowledge that they are "fearfully and wonderfully made" (Psalm 139:14). The constant lash of the parental tongue, or the persistent neglect of care for the child, eventually would bind and shrivel their inner person, making it seem incongruous that they are a wonder of God's creation. Yet these people are among those for whom God's care is such that "A bruised reed he will not break" (Isaiah 42:3); such is His tenderness, consideration and acknowledgement for all, including those whose lives from their early childhood are marred and damaged.

As an aside, there are a few kinds of reeds named in the bible including the water reed, a writing reed and the stronger reed, *Arundo donax*, known as the giant reed. The giant reed has been cultivated throughout Asia, southern Europe, northern Africa, and the Middle East for thousands of years. Its tall canes contain silica, giving the plant firmness such that the reeds are useful as supports for climbing plants and vines; even serving as fishing rods and walking sticks. Hence, a bruised reed is of limited use. It has lost its potential strength and stiffness. Yet, such a reed, seemingly useless, God will protect and does not discard.

Having given examples of where the captivation and preoccupation with earthly glory is a path away from God, damaging many along its lure of earthly ascent, some opposite examples are worth noting. These positive examples are people in scripture who were imbued with earthly glory, yet their primary focus lay not with their own glory; but rather they looked to God and were not chiefly reliant on their personal glory. Three examples are considered: Esther, the Centurion, and the apostle Paul.

Esther

Esther was an orphan, raised by her elder cousin Mordecai. Esther was Mordecai's uncle's daughter. Her Jewish name Hadassah means "myrtle" and her Persian name Esther means "star". Mordecai raised Esther as if she was his daughter and he greatly cared for her. She was a stunning physical beauty. She is described with Hebrew words we translate as "fair and beautiful" (Esther 2:7). Literally, the Hebrew words mean "beautiful in form and lovely to look at."

The magnificence of her beauty was revealed through a search for a new queen for the Persian King Xerxes. The selection process involved a countrywide beauty pageant. A harem of Persia's most beautiful women was assembled. The ancient Jewish historian Josephus says the king had 400 women selected.

The Book of Esther recounts how Esther, a resident of Susa, the nation's capital, was included in the selection. The king had appointed commissioners in each of the 127 provinces to identify "beautiful young virgins" (Esther 2:2) to be brought to Susa. Being Babylon's capital, Susa would have contained thousands of eligible girls, so the chances of a local girl being selected as the representative of the province in which the capital Susa was located would be slight. Nonetheless Esther was selected, indicative of the rarity of her beauty, and she found favour with Hegai (Esther 2:3,8,9), the king's eunuch, who was in charge of the harem. He gave her special food and beauty treatments. He also gave her seven choice maidservants and moved her and her maidservants into "the best place in the harem" (Esther 2:9).

Persia was a country famous for its aromatic perfumes and bridal preparation customs, including ritualistic baths, plucking of eyebrows, painting of hands and feet with henna, facial make-up, and applications of a beautifying paste all over the body, meant to lighten the colour of the skin and remove spots and blemishes. The ancient Hebrew word for beauty preparations comes from the root "to scour, and to polish."

The beauty preparation for each virgin lasted twelve months. A possible practical reason for this length of preparation was to ensure that the women truly were virgins, as any pregnancy would have become obvious during that period of bodily scrutiny and preparation.

The destiny of each woman and her chance to be queen initially rested on one evening with the king. Following that single evening, "She would not return to the king unless he was pleased with her and summoned her by name." (Esther 2:14). Fortunately "Esther won the favour of everyone who saw her" (Esther 2:15) and "the king was attracted to Esther more than to any of the other women, and she won his favour and approval more than any of the other virgins. So he set a royal crown on her head and made her queen" (Esther 2:17). As for the other 399 girls, they were banished to the harem where they stayed as concubines of the king, and rarely if ever saw him afterwards. They were never free to marry another man, essentially living as perpetual widows.

After the selection of Esther as queen, the Book of Esther then continues the story describing how the king greatly honoured a nobleman named Haman. Yet, for reasons explained in the book, Haman subsequently sought the destruction of the Jewish people and convinced the king of this necessity. However, the king was unaware that his queen Esther was a Jewess. In order to eventually plead to the king that the Jewish exiles, who included herself, should not be exterminated required Esther risking her life by appearing unannounced before the king (Esther 4:11-16). Any person who dared to appear unannounced in the king's presence was subject to execution, unless the king specifically signalled his acceptance of their uninvited interruption to the proceedings of his court.

The risk Esther was prepared to take was no small risk. The king was not averse to being annoyed and he was known to express his displeasure in brutal ways. One illustration was that when a storm destroyed the bridge by which he would cross into Greece, he commanded the engineers to be slain, and then had the sea beaten with chains to subdue it into 'better manners'.

What is worth noting about Esther is that her knowledge of her beauty did not sour into arrogance, cunning, conceit and self-pride. She regularly listened to the counsel of her fatherly cousin Mordecai. She listened to and accepted the advice of Hegai, the keeper of the harem. She confided in her inner circle of servants and sought their involvement in her personal life beyond the palace. The glory and acclaim of her great physical beauty was not something she worshipped. She remained a Jewess, alert to being an obedient and caring daughter.

In preparing to appear unannounced before the king, to provide an opportunity to petition for the Jewish community, she first fasted as a Jew, in the company of fasting Jews (Esther 4:11-16). In doing so, she sought not to preserve her own life or beauty, but risked it all for the sake of preserving the lives of God's people, the Jews throughout Persia. The act of fasting (Esther 4:16) reveals that she chose not to place her reliance in the glory of her beauty but rather in honour and servitude to God. Physical beauty was not the vain idol in which she gloried but rather her foremost desire was to be a daughter of the Lord God.

Esther is a positive example of personal glory not worshipped. Her primary motivation was not to preserve her status as queen or her remarkable physical beauty. Rather she sought to preserve her people and to serve God's people. She was prepared to be respectfully vulnerable, and avoided being consumed by the arrogance of power, prestige and natural beauty.

The Centurion

Luke 7:1-10 tells the story of the centurion whose servant was exceedingly ill and, through Jewish elders, he asked Jesus to heal his servant. Due to his military rank, the centurion knew power, knew authority, and knew physical might and dominance. His skill, might and leadership qualities would have underpinned his rise up through the ranks. He could so easily have been like some ambitious others; a person consumed by arrogance and the status of power. He could so easily have succumbed to a self-serving pursuit of the glory of military status and self-aggrandizement through his authority, power and dominance over many, but he apparently did not.

He was not culturally aloof. He "highly valued" his sick Jewish servant and sought care for him. As a centurion, he could have exercised his authority and might and ordered Christ be brought to him. Rather he respectfully sought out the Jewish elders and asked that they approach Christ. He also chose not to lavish his wealth solely on himself for he had built a synagogue for the local Jewish community (Luke 7:5).

Although he respected his status as a centurion, he chose in this instance to reside his confidence in Christ, His ability to heal and the power of His word. The centurion chose not to directly order Christ to come to him, nor to pay for the healing services of Christ. Moreover, the centurion already knew that he was unworthy to receive Christ in person. That is why his request to Christ was via the Jewish elders.

It is interesting that the Jewish elders requested Christ to heal the centurion's servant not because they, unlike the centurion, recognised Christ's status and power. Rather their request to Christ was based on the status and actions of the centurion. In their eyes, the commendable acts of the centurion and his status were sufficient reasons for Christ to act. Yet, in contrast, the centurion was already persuaded by the power and status of Christ, not his own power, status or acts. He already knew that, although a centurion, he was unworthy to approach Christ. Hence, the centurion says to Christ through servants, "I did not consider myself worthy to come to you. But say the word, and my servant will be healed." (Luke 7:8).

Christ notes that the centurion places confidence in Him, His power and His authority. The centurion has a confidence that Christ will listen to him, in spite of him being a Gentile, and that Christ has the power to heal and that His word is power, being sufficient to cause healing. The centurion already knows that his own status, wealth and actions cannot be the source of healing. The way the centurion resides confidence in Christ causes Christ to express amazement. It is the only time recorded in the New Testament where Christ expresses positive amazement and He says to the crowd around Him "I tell you, I have not found such great faith even in Israel."

The centurion is a great illustration of faith, a God-given gift that frees a person to place unswerving trust and credence in God. The centurion, blessed by rank, authority, wealth and physical might chose not to focus on those aspects of his glory. Rather, he focused on the needs of his servant and the power and prowess of Christ.

Paul

Much is known about Paul. Some other things can be inferred or judged as likely, given what is known of the times and cultures in which he lived. We know his father was a Pharisee and that the family's tent-making business was sufficiently commercially successful to allow the family to send Paul to be educated in Jerusalem in the famous Hillel Pharisaic school under the tutelage of Gamaliel, the grandson of Hillel, the school's founder. Paul's family held the coveted status of Citizen of Rome. Such citizenship conferred local distinction and ensured hereditary privileges. Later in his life, Paul made use of this citizenship.

Pollock (1969) comments how Paul as a student would have learned to debate in the question-and-answer style known to the ancient world as the diatribe. Paul would also have learned how to expound the texts of Mosaic law and the books of the prophets. As revealed in the letters he would later dictate and send to the various newly established churches in Asia Minor and Greece, Paul was deeply familiar with the scriptures we now call the Old Testament. His extensive knowledge was accompanied by great passion, as evidenced by the eagerness and persistence with which he persecuted followers of Jesus, judging them to be corrupted and plagued by heresy. He was determined to remove the stain of the Jesus movement and so sought to destroy it; "Going from house to house, he dragged off men and women and put them in prison." (Acts 8:3).

Of his prowess, Paul says later in a letter to the churches in Galatia, "I was advancing in Judaism beyond many Jews of my own age, and was extremely jealous for the traditions of my fathers." (Galatians 1:13). Acts 9:1,2 describes how "He went to the high priest and asked him for letters to the synagogues in Damascus, so that if he found any there who belonged to the Way, whether men or women, he might take them as prisoners to Jerusalem."

It is worth pausing at this point to reflect on the nature and calibre of Paul. He had great energy and determination, coupled with an authority provided by a prestigious education, culminating in an acknowledged prowess among his peers. His zeal, authority and severity of action created a lasting fearful reputation among the followers of Christ (Acts 9:21, 26). Paul was energetic, influential, scholastically pre-eminent and ambitious. These are often socially attractive traits and Paul could so easily have gloried in their possession and display. The colloquial expression is that he could so easily have been 'full of himself'.

Whether Paul, as Saul the Pharisee, gloried in his achievements and attributes, we cannot fully know. What we are more confident to say is that, following his conversion and years of preparation for his missionary journeys, Paul remained energetic and deeply knowledgeable about the scriptures. Yet his focus was not on exercising his status and power as a Pharisee; but rather as a servant of Christ (Philippians 1:1, Romans 1:1).

Following years of service, he was able to write honestly of himself and his companions stating that they did not seek glory (i.e. praise) from people. In addition, they did not place financial demands or burdens on those they taught (1 Thessalonians 2:6,7). Even though Paul was imbued with a prestigious array of talents that he could use for his own ends; he chose not to do so. Paul's talents, energy and authority were some of the ingredients of his earthly glory, setting him apart from many others. However, he chose not to be pre-occupied and obsessed with his own glory (i.e. fame, acclaim, praise, boasting). He wrote, "I glory in Christ Jesus in my service to God." (Romans 5:17) and so advised others that "whatever you do, do it all to the glory of God." (1 Corinthians 10:31).

Therefore, in summary, Esther, the centurion and Saint Paul were people imbued with earthly glory yet their primary focus lay not with their own glory; but rather they looked to God. They were reliant on His care and authority, and were not reliant on their personal prowess — their earthly glory.

Actions "for the glory of God"

The apostle Paul, in his letter to the Romans, writes that there are those who do not solely act for their own human glory but rather act for God's glory, always endeavouring to act rightly, such that the outcome is praise of God not praise of the individual. Paul writes of God's response to such people: "To those who by persistence in doing good seek glory, honor and immortality, he will give eternal life." (Romans 2:7). Importantly, however, to do something "for the glory of God" does NOT mean that God's glory depends on us as if we somehow by our actions determine the magnitude of God's glory. God's glory is His property NOT the property of our actions. God's glory is not an accounting column in which we add to God's glory by our actions.

We are NOT the determinants of God's glory. Glory in His property.

God is not weak. He is not like a frail elderly person who needs response from us, who is made stronger or happier by us supposing we can add to His glory. God is not dependent on us in the sense that He needs us to do things for Him. Doing something for His glory is not an action to fill a need in God. The shepherd is not dependent on the sheep. It is the sheep that need the protection and guidance of the shepherd. He is the Good Shepherd and we are the sheep (Psalm 78:52; Ezekiel 34:11; John 10:11-15). We may be "wonderfully made" but we are not the Originator of the wonder.

Glory is not like a gift that we can buy or fashion and then give to God in order to increase His glory. Thus, when we say, "Give glory to God", it does not mean that somehow our actions can enlarge God's greatness or abundance, His glory. Rather to give glory to God or to act for the glory of God is to give to Him our _reaction_. God's glory is <u>His</u> glory; it is not conditional on our actions. Glory is God's nature — "Salvation and glory and power belong to our God," (Revelation 19:1).

Remember He first loved us, not vice versa. To give Him glory is not our initiative. It is our _reaction_, based on our acknowledgement of Him. It is in response to all that He is and all that He has done. Remember that when Jesus taught the disciples to pray, the first words He encouraged them to use were "Our Father", in recognition of God's actions and status. The only 'actions' of ours stipulated in the Lord's prayer are "as we also have forgiven our debtors".

To give glory to God, in the words of Albert Barnes, "is to acknowledge him as the only true God; to set up his pure worship in the heart; and to praise him as the great Ruler of heaven and earth." (See Barnes' notes on Revelation 14:7). People can praise or glorify Christ for various reasons and with a range of motivations. However, our individual glorification by God is accomplished only because Christ dwells in those He glorifies. The portal of faith is _reaction_ to God, not a retinue of actions or activities. On this side of Eden, actions and activities can have all manner of godly and ungodly motivations. Christ said, "If anyone serves Me, he must follow Me; and where I am, My servant will be as well. If anyone serves Me, the Father will honour him." (John 12:26).

I repeat His words that stress reaction; "he must *follow Me*". Following Christ is a reaction to Him and His leading. From that, reaction does come other actions, which together constitute serving Him. Graciously, in reciprocation, God promises that He will honour us. His honour, His glory He showers on us.

Lastly, to say the same but in the negative — just as we cannot increase God's glory neither can we diminish it. As C.S. Lewis once wrote, "A man can no more diminish God's glory by refusing to worship Him than a lunatic can put out the sun by scribbling the word, 'darkness' on the walls of his cell." God's glory is immutable, changeless. We cannot quench, erode or diminish it. Neither can our actions enlarge it. It is His glory, not ours to influence. Remember the transfiguration of Christ. The actions of Peter, James and John in no way caused or altered Christ's glory. That glory was impressive, incandescent and arresting; and made no more or less by what the three disciples said or did.

The effect of God's glory

God's glory affects us. Because it is a visible display of His magnificence, God's glory often creates in people responses of awe, fear, wonder or anxiety. At the transfiguration Peter, James and John "saw his glory" (Luke 9:32). Their response was to be very frightened (Mark 9:6). The writer of Matthew's gospel says, "they fell face down to the ground, terrified." (Matthew 17:6). At the time of Christ's birth, when the angel of the Lord appeared at night to the shepherds, "the glory of the Lord shone around them, and they were terrified." (Luke 2:9). When "the glory of the Lord settled on Mount Sinai" (Exodus 24:15), "To the Israelites the glory of the Lord looked like a consuming fire". (Exodus 24:17). On another occasion also involving Moses and the Israelites, "the glory of the Lord appeared to all the people." (Leviticus 9:23) and then "Fire came out from the presence of the Lord....And when all the people saw it, they shouted for joy and fell face down." (Leviticus 9:24). When Jesus turned the water into wine, the apostle John described how "He thus revealed his glory" (John 2:11b) which triggered a response of faith in Christ by the disciples present. Christ's power and care was expressed by not only turning water into wine, but turning it into the best wine, certainly as judged by the master of the wedding banquet (John 2:8-10).

The glory of God is sufficiently powerful to alter, at least temporarily, not only a person's physical position but also demeanour. By illustration, the exposure to God's glory can leave people prostrate (Matthew 17:6; Acts 9:3-4). In addition and only mentioned once in the Old Testament is that exposure to God's glory can physically alter a person. The case is that of Moses whose exposure to God's glory left Moses with a gradually fading brightness of his face. Moses "was not aware that his face was radiant because he had spoken with the LORD." (Exodus 34:29). The after-glow was so striking that Aaron and all other Israelites were afraid to approach Moses (Exodus 34:30).

Although the glory of God is forceful and brilliant, it does not alter a person's nature. Our inner nature is summed up in the maxim "All have sinned" (Romans 3:23). That is our nature. We are sinful. Consider the example of the apostle Peter. Before the transfiguration, he was a sinful man. Peter already knew this because by the lakeside when he prostrated himself before Christ, Peter said, "Go away from me, Lord; I am a sinful man!" (Luke 5:8). Much later, he experienced God's glory at the transfiguration. Was his sinful nature altered by that experience? No! After the transfiguration, Peter remained a sinful man. Three times he lied about having any association with Christ (Luke 22:54-61), in spite of openly saying to Christ just a few hours earlier, "Lord, I am ready to go with you to prison and to death." (Luke 22:33). Another illustration is Moses and Aaron (Number 20:6-12). Despite the glory of the Lord appearing to them (Numbers 20:6) and God instructing them carefully about what to do and say (Numbers 20:8), Moses and Aaron failed to follow God's instructions. By failing to honour and trust God, Moses and Aaron were forbidden by God to lead the Israelites into the Promised Land. Their exposure to God's glory did not prevent their disobedience.

Exposure to God's glory is part of God's communication that He is who He says He is. Yet despite the immediacy and even longer-term impacts of exposure to God's glory, a person's inner nature (their legal core) is not altered. All remain marred by sin with the result being a spiritual death, separation from God (Romans 6:23). All remain exposed to God's rightful judgement. All remain in need of forgiveness, purification and renewal, if they are to stand and last in God's presence. Being exposed to God's glory or being knowledgeable about Him is not an admission ticket to heaven. The gateway to heaven is reliance on the saving act of Christ for "the gift of God is eternal life in Christ Jesus our Lord." (Romans 6:23).

Although exposure to God's glory does not change our nature, the exposure is nonetheless memorable. Events that are unusual and remarkable are often memorable. For Peter the transfiguration was a powerful reality that stayed with him. Remembering the event was a source of confidence and comfort; not re-lived fear and unease (2 Peter 1:17-18).

The demise of earthly glory

So attractive is earthly glory and praise that its loss through ageing, accident, disease or misfortune can propel a person into sorrow, depression, grieving, anger and resignation. If a person cannot eventually accept the loss or erosion of their earthly glory, they risk bitterness of spirit, a resentment, a sullenness or disengagement. Loss of earthly glory can strip a person of their dignity, comfort and their perceived usefulness to others, leading them to wish for, and in some cases actively to seek death.

It is no surprise that in some communities, especially in those where wealth, youthfulness, ability and utility are paramount, an appetite for euthanasia arises. For some the loss of glory (ability, status, achievement, wealth, beauty) is so great and the attendant misery or fear of being a financial burden so powerful that death is sought.

There are some among us, who from birth, due to genetic abnormality or other conditions have impaired physical or mental earthly glory. They are incapacitated, or limited in body or mind. To our ear and eye they are not "wonderfully made" and there may be no remedy to their condition. Daily around them is the display of the talent and beauty of others that incessantly reminds them that, by contrast, they lack earthly glory.

God's promise to these folk, weakened from the start of their lives and sometimes limping to its end, is that that they will receive from Him great tenderness and a magnitude of care we could never match. "He will not crush the weakest reed or put out a flickering candle." (Isaiah 42:3, New Living Translation).

The societal emphasis on physical beauty leads many seeking to prolong or enhance their physical attractiveness. The pressure on women to be physically attractive is pronounced in most societies. In richer countries, much expenditure occurs on personal services, grooming, cosmetics and surgical enhancements in order to increase or prolong the glory of physical beauty.

We live in environments where the toil and anxiety of work and family life inevitably will leave their psychological and physical marks upon us. The power of the sun in some countries will blemish and wrinkle us. Age will weary us and sap us of strength and attractiveness. We will grow weaker eventually, and many of our skills and abilities will diminish, atrophy or cease.

Despite our reasonable or extravagant endeavours, our earthly glory of beauty and skill will lessen.

Glorification

In his mammoth treatise on Paul's letter to the Romans, Lloyd-Jones (1970) makes the sobering observation that:

> "It is surely significant that there has been virtually no emphasis on glorification, especially during the past century; and yet this is the thing to which the Apostle directs attention at the very beginning of chapter 5 and which he unfolds to us in such glowing terms in chapter 8, and especially the certainty of it all." (p. 7).

His observation, in my view, easily could apply to the many decades since he wrote that statement. Few homilies and sermons expound glory and glorification. Perhaps more pointedly, when the topics of justification by faith and sanctification are raised, rarely is the topic of glorification given equivalent prominence, and sometimes it goes unmentioned. Yet Paul often links all these topics. For example, In Romans 5:1-2 he writes:

> "Therefore, since we have been justified through faith, we have peace with God through our Lord Jesus Christ, through whom we have gained access by faith into this grace in which we now stand. And we rejoice in the hope of the glory of God."

Note these two verses start by mentioning our justification through faith, yet end with the hope of the glory of God.

Also, consider Romans 8:30 where Paul writes:

> "And those he predestined, he also called; those he called,
> he also justified; those he justified, he also glorified."

In this verse, again Paul links justification with glorification. First, justification; then glorification. Not only has God provided His gift of Christ's work of salvation, claimed through justification by faith, but God also has in store for us glorification, being fitted to be in His presence where He is.

What is the nature of glorification?

Firstly, glorification is the continuance of our walk with God. The Psalmist writes:

> "You guide me with your counsel and afterwards you
> will take me into glory. Whom have I in heaven but you?
> And being with you, I desire nothing on earth." (Psalm
> 73:24-25).

God, our heavenly Father, counsels us, and then leads us, His children, into the embrace of heaven, to be in His company. The apostle Paul echoes the same sentiment when writing to the church at Colossae:

> "Since, then, you have been raised with Christ, set your
> hearts on things above, where Christ is seated at the
> right hand of God. Set your minds on things above, not
> on earthly things. For you died, and your life is now
> hidden with Christ in God. When Christ, who is your
> life, appears, then you also will appear with him in glory."
> (Colossians 3:1-4)

Just as Christ, the good shepherd, led the three up the mount to experience glory, so His Father, the LORD God, will lead each of His children into the wonder of heaven, the eternal glory (2 Timothy 2:10).

The journey into heaven is via a process of sanctification and purification. Spurgeon (1883) says:

"We cannot be glorified so long as sin remains in us; we must first be pardoned, renewed, and sanctified, and then we are fitted to be glorified."

In a similar vein, Lloyd-Jones (1975) writes:

"Glorification is the ultimate end and goal of salvation; and we must never stop short of it. We must never think of our Christian position as merely one of being forgiven. That is but the beginning of it, it is not the end. Even sanctification is not the end. The end is glorification." (p2).

The 19th century commentator, Albert Barnes, said of Moses and Elijah "who appeared in glory" (Luke 9:31) that their appearance was like that "which the saints have in heaven." This comment by Barnes is consistent with a later statement by F. F. Bruce (1964) who says, "glory is sanctification completed." (p. 178). This link between glory and sanctification is illustrated in Isaiah 6:3 that describes angels crying, "Holy, holy, holy is the LORD almighty" — the next thing these angels say is — "The whole earth is full of his glory." Note you might expect this verse, having begun by stating that God is holy, would end with a statement that the earth is full of his holiness; but no, it ends with the statement that "the whole earth is full of his glory." This suggests that glory is the visible outpouring of His holiness, with the core of His magnificence being His holiness. Hence, glory is the visible manifestation of God's holiness, His magnificence, His power, His nature and His person.

Secondly, glorification is the precedent and aftermath of a discernment and a reckoning. Matthew 25:31-34 starkly states:

"When the Son of Man comes in his glory, and all the angels with him, he will sit on his glorious throne. All the nations will be gathered before him, and he will separate the people one from another as a shepherd separates the sheep from the goats. He will put the sheep on his right and the goats on his left. Then the King will say to those on his right, 'Come, you who are blessed by my Father; take your inheritance, the kingdom prepared for you since the creation of the world.'"

Notice, this passage begins with expression of God's glory "When the Son of Man comes in his glory" and ends with the glory of being in His presence, in His kingdom "Come, you who are blessed by my Father; take your inheritance, the kingdom prepared for you."

In Matthew's gospel, almost the entirety of chapter 13 is a sequence of parables about the kingdom of heaven. Christ explains some of the meanings of those parables to His disciples and we as readers are privy to those explanations. Some other parables have no accompanying explanation and other means must be found to distil their meaning. What is clear from some of the parables is that the journey to heaven and its glory is conditional on discerning what is truly valuable, lastingly, incalculably valuable. The journey to heaven is also via a reckoning, a judgement; a separating. "Everything is uncovered and laid bare before the eyes of him to whom we must give account." (Hebrews 4:13). The apostle Paul comments: "each of us will give an account of himself to God." (Romans 14:12). C.S. Lewis says this same thing more eloquently than ever I will:

> "In the end that Face which is the delight or the terror of the universe must be turned upon each of us either with one expression or with the other, either conferring glory inexpressible or inflicting shame that can never be cured or disguised." (p. 10, Weight of Glory)[3]

The parables in chapter 13 of Matthew's gospel tell of weeds being separated from wheat, and a fishing haul requiring good fish to be piled apart from bad fish. The weeds are burned whilst the separated wheat is brought into the landowner's barn. The good fish are retained in baskets, while the bad are discarded. There is a reckoning. There is a judgement. There is a separating. Not all seek or enter the kingdom of heaven.

---

[3] The Weight of Glory by C.S. Lewis copyright C.S. Lewis Pte. Ltd. 1949. Extract reprinted by permission.

As an aside, the characteristics of fish Jewish fishermen would deem as "bad" are defined in the book of Leviticus 11:9-12 as:

> "Of all the creatures living in the water of the seas and the streams, you may eat any that have fins and scales. But all creatures in the seas or streams that do not have fins and scales—whether among all the swarming things or among all the other living creatures in the water—you are to detest. And since you are to detest them, you must not eat their meat and you must detest their carcasses. Anything living in the water that does not have fins and scales is to be detestable to you."

A fish without scales found in the Sea of Galilee is the bottom-dwelling catfish. It was judged as unclean, not to be eaten.

Associated with the return of Christ in glory is that each person will be judged and rewarded. Revelation 22:12 quotes Christ saying, "I will give to everyone according to what he has done". Our actions, motivations and attitudes matter to God. He is our judge. Thus, glorification is the precedent and aftermath of a reckoning, a judgement.

Yet to experience glorification is also the aftermath of discernment. At Golgotha one of the two criminals crucified near Christ called out to Him; "Jesus, remember me when you come into your kingdom." (Luke 23:42). Even near death, this man registered his need of Christ. Immediately, Christ answered him; "I tell you the truth, today you will be with me in paradise." (Luke 23:43). Discernment of his need of Christ meant his glorification was the aftermath.

When speaking to the multitude and outlining the meaning and nature of blessedness (Matthew 5:1-12; Luke 6:17-23), Jesus commenced by saying: "Blessed are the poor in spirit, for theirs is the kingdom of heaven" (Matthew 5:3). Those enabled to be aware of their spiritual poverty, who are given and accept that discernment, have the blessing of the prospect of heaven, being glorified, sharing in God's glory. It is our loving Father "who is able to keep you from falling and to present you before his glorious presence without fault and with great joy." (Jude 24).

It is interesting to note that the first feature of blessedness that

Christ highlighted is that the person has awareness of their spiritual impoverishment before God, yet simultaneously is aware of their legal status with God. They are citizens of heaven, sharing in the glory of heaven where resides their heavenly Father.

Although experiencing glorification is the aftermath of discernment, the experience of God's glory is not always the aftermath of discernment. The shepherds living out in the fields when Christ was born had no initial discernment of their need of Him. Their routine was abruptly altered when an angel of the Lord appeared to them and God's glory shone around them (Luke 2:8,9). Soon after, there suddenly appeared a great company of the host of heaven saying, "Glory to God in the highest, and on earth peace to men on whom his favour rests." (Luke 2: 14,14).

Having said that the experience of God's glory is not always the aftermath of discernment, nonetheless the experience of God's glory can occur after discernment of His status or our need of Him. For example, it was after the disciples discerned Jesus to be the Christ (i.e. messiah) (Luke 9:18-22) that Christ then led them up the mount to witness His glory. Another example is Stephen who, soon to be stoned, looked heavenward "and saw the glory of God, and Jesus standing at the right hand of God." (Acts 7: 55).

Thirdly, to be glorified is to be made pure. Revelation 21:27 says of heaven, the New Jerusalem, that "Nothing impure will ever enter it". Our glorification in heaven is only possible because of the purification Christ has provided. Purification is the precursor of glorification. Christ has "provided purification for sins" (Hebrews 1:3). God the Father has raised Him from the dead and glorified Him (1 Peter 1:21). God in judgement is a purifier, a refiner, causing separation of the precious from the dross, thereby creating purity (Malachi 3:2-3).

It is often the case that we understate the purifying work of Christ; yet the Old Testament contains much description of purification practices, highlighting the differences between uncleanliness and cleanliness. Those that were to stand and serve in the tabernacle and temple needed to undergo purification. To be in God's presence required purity, being unsullied, without stain or blemish.

The visual references to God's actions requiring and producing purity include the practice of refining metal (Malachi 3:2-3) or cleansing cloth

(Malachi 3:2). There is much imagery describing the whiteness of robes or the dazzling whiteness and brightness of angelic appearances, indicative of purity. Purification involved cleansing; preserving what was precious whilst removing all that stained and weakened.

Spurgeon writes:

> "God's Holy Spirit, when He has finished His work, will leave in us no trace of sin; no temptation shall be able to touch us, there will be in us no relics of our past and fallen state." (p. 247, Day by Day with C.H. Spurgeon)

We read in 1 John 1:9; "If we confess our sins, he is faithful and just and will forgive us our sins and purify us from all unrighteousness." In Isaiah, we read where God says, "I will thoroughly purge away your dross and remove your impurities." (Isaiah 1:25b). Those in Christ will stand before God. Through Christ, they are made and judged righteous, acceptable to God. They are made pure and blameless, with all their dross and blemish of sin removed. Lloyd-Jones (1975) comments how "The whole man will be completely and entirely delivered from every harmful effect of sin, every tarnishing, polluting effect of sin." (p2).

One of David's psalms was written after the prophet Nathan confronted David concerning his adultery with Bathsheba and the death of Uriah that David had planned. In acknowledging his guilt and need of God's care, David says, "Cleanse me with hyssop, and I shall be clean; wash me, and I shall be whiter than snow." (Psalm 51:7). David plainly reveals his need to be purified, cleansed and made acceptable to God. He also noted that such purification was only possible by the work of God.

Another aspect of purification is that it enables our interaction with God and one another to be untarnished. In heaven, hesitancy, regret or crippling fear in our communication with God and one another is absent; for we are purified, welcomed and loved as the brothers and sisters of God's family. Contrast that with our earthly interactions with one another where hidden agendas, pride, envy, malice, lust and dishonesty are mingled with all that is commendable. Sometimes we speak too much or too little. At times, we are too unkind in our speaking. We ignore speaking plainly, when we should. We fail to listen or we hear what we want to hear. We are too defensive or too offensive. We verbally destroy when we should build. These difficulties, aberrations and weaknesses, which impair our earthly communications with one another, are not carried into heaven. We are purified and enabled to hear and speak with perfect clarity, fuelled by the purity of God's Spirit and intention. We are untrammelled by our past for we are made anew; with all our dross and weakness removed.

At the transfiguration, when Moses, Elijah and the Christ were in earnest discussion, there was no dissent, unease or disillusionment. The Greek word that describes their interaction, συλλαλοῦντες (Mark 9:4), means 'to talk together'. It was not a lecture or discourse. It was genuine shared discussion. There was confidence, empathy and clarity; for us a glimpse of the future in His company.

Fourthly, glorification involves changes in the nature and appearance of our bodily form. In Christ, we are forgiven but we are not left forever unchanged, with bodies permanently marred and weakened by sin. God's gift of glorification purifies and transforms us. We receive new bodies never subject to decay. As Lloyd-Jones (1975) says, "Glorification means full and entire deliverance from sin and evil in all their effects and in every respect —body, soul and spirit." (p. 2).

The transfiguration provided a glimpse of those who had died but were now spiritually anew. In the presence of Christ, conversing with Him were Elijah and Moses. The bodies of Moses and Elijah were similar yet different to human bodies. Similar inasmuch as they had a human form and movement easily recognised as persons by James, John and Peter. Similar insofar as they were capable of conversation; hearing, speaking and comprehending (Luke 9:31). However, different insofar as they could appear (Mark 9:4) and disappear in an instant (Mark 9:8). Different in that their bodies were associated with a glorious splendour (Luke 9:31), or as Barnes notes, "Of an appearance like that which the saints have in heaven."

The facility of appearing and disappearing was later similarly evidenced by the risen Christ. After the long interaction with the two disciples walking to Emmaus, and after sharing bread together, he "disappeared from their sight." (Luke 24:31). He also twice appeared to a larger group of the disciples as they sat fearfully behind locked doors (John 20:19, John 20:26). Sometime later, in full sight of His disciples, "While he was blessing them, he left them and was taken up into heaven." (Luke 24:51).

C. H. Spurgeon's view about the nature of the resurrected body is as follows:

> "The body of a child will be fully developed, and the dwarf will attain to full stature. The blind shall not be sightless in heaven, neither shall the lame be halt, nor shall the palsied tremble. The deaf shall hear, and the dumb shall sing God's praises. We shall carry none of our deficiencies or infirmities to heaven . . . neither shall any of us need a staff to lean upon. There we shall not know an aching groan or a weak knee or a failing eye. 'The inhabitants shall no more say, I am sick.'" (Sermon No 1721, The Charles Spurgeon Sermon Collection (1834-1893))

If we think of the behaviour of Christ during his earthly sojourn then there is some sympathy for Spurgeon's view, as Christ remedied many ailments such as blindness, deafness, lameness and withered limbs.

Subsequently, Spurgeon says the resurrected body shall be:

> "a body that will be incapable of any kind of suffering: no palpitating heart, no sinking spirit, no aching limbs, no lethargic soul shall worry us there. No, we shall be perfectly delivered from every evil of that kind. Moreover, it shall be an immortal body. Our risen bodies shall not be capable of decay, much less of death. There are no graves in glory. Blessed are the dead that died in the Lord, for their bodies shall rise never to know death and corruption a second time." (as quoted by Northrop (2004)).

Yet for all the purification and alteration in our form that makes us fit for heaven, to be in God's company, treated and known as a member of Christ's family, there will nonetheless be something of our form that makes us recognised from the days of old when we lived on earth. The risen Christ was in form different, inasmuch as He could miraculously appear, disappear and be lifted into the air without support (Luke 24: 51; Acts 1:9). However, He was able to be recognised by His actions (John

21: 5-12), in the way he broke bread (Luke 24: 30,31), by the marks of the crucifixion He continued to bear (John 20:20) and by His general appearance (Matthew 28: 17). He was no stranger to those who knew Him. The same is likely for us. We will be somehow recognizable to those known to us.

A glorified body is not simply a revived earthly body but rather it is a spiritual body, a purified body fully and solely animated by God's Spirit; the same Spirit that produces love, joy, peace, patience, kindness, goodness, faithfulness, gentleness and self-control (Galatians 5:22,23). Earthly bodies are perishable, subject to disgrace, tiring and weakness (1 Corinthians 15:42–53), whereas glorified bodies are imperishable, honourable, enduring and powerful.

Just as our earthly bodies are suited to life on earth, so resurrected bodies will be fit for life in heaven. Resurrected bodies will have form and solidity to the touch, yet travel is seamless and unencumbered (John 20:19, 26; Luke 24:39).

A glimpse of a resurrection body is shown in Jesus' post-resurrection appearances. He still had visible but purified wounds, and His disciples could physically touch Him and His painless wounds. He could travel effortlessly and appear or disappear at will. He could pass through walls and doors yet could also eat, drink, walk, sit and talk. Scripture informs us that our "lowly bodies" will be just "like His glorious body" (Philippians 3:21). The decay and impairment of our physical status that can constrain how we may want physically to serve God and those placed in our care while on earth will be forever gone, freeing us to praise, serve and glorify Him for eternity.

As to when glorification and the return of Christ will exactly occur, all that need be said is that, although anticipated and wished for by many, it will nonetheless still occur as a surprise. The apostle Peter comments; "But the day of the Lord will come like a thief. The heavens will disappear with a roar; the elements will be destroyed by fire, and the earth and everything in it will be laid bare. …. But in keeping with his promise we are looking forward to a new heaven and a new earth, the home of righteousness." (2 Peter 3:10,13).

Those believers in Christ who are alive when Christ returns will have the benefit of their bodies being immediately transformed and purified.

Their glorified bodies will not be their earthly bodies of flesh and blood for "Flesh and blood cannot inherit the kingdom of God." (1 Corinthians 15:50). Each glorified body will be a spiritual body; visible, perfect and powerful, not a translucent phantom, not plagued by fatigue, nor sorrow, nor hunger, nor thirst, nor tears (Revelation 7:16-17; Revelation 21:4). Lloyd-Jones (1975) comments, "we shall be perfect and entire in every respect, spiritually, morally, physically, bodily." (p.73). He later says, "we shall be delivered forever from all the things that have ever caused us misery or unhappiness or pain or sorrow. That is our destiny." (p.74). Even later he adds, "Body, soul, spirit, entirely, utterly, absolutely delivered from sin and all its effects and all its vestiges!" (p.89).

Fifthly, glorification is the product of relationship; as brief as that between the crucified criminal and Christ, yet often fortunately longer. Glorification is the final outworking of God's care for those who rely on Christ, and through such faith in Him, they have an immutable change in their status with God. They are family, as revealed by the writer of Hebrews:

> "Both the one who makes people holy and those who are
> made holy are of the same family. So Jesus is not ashamed
> to call them brothers and sisters." (Hebrews 2:11).

It is no surprise that Jesus taught His disciples to pray first "Our Father in heaven..". This is the legal and emotional language of the status of family. God, in heaven, is our Father. Jesus, His Son, calls those with a residing confidence in God, His brothers and sisters. These relationships legally define our standing with God, when we are enabled to place trust in Him. He is our Father, in heaven. We are His children, residing on earth; yet to be in His presence in heaven.

Glorification is the product of being welcomed, being noticed by God. Again, to quote from C.S. Lewis:

"Perhaps it seems rather crude to describe glory as the fact of being "noticed" by God. But this is almost the language of the New Testament." (p. 11, Weight of Glory).[4]

Glorification arises from being 'noticed' and welcomed by God as a member of Christ's family, for "Jesus is not ashamed to call them brothers". He says:

"In My Father's house are many rooms. If it were not so, would I have told you that I am going there to prepare a place for you? And if I go and prepare a place for you, I will come back and welcome you into My presence, so that *you also may be where I am.*" (John 14:2-3).

Sixthly, glorification is a gift of inheritance. The apostle Paul in his letter to the church in Rome makes clear that all Christians are heirs of God, and joint-heirs with Christ (Romans 8:16-17). God's gift, the inheritance He shares, is life everlasting with Him; to be with Him in His glorious presence. We already have a glimpse of this future with Elijah and Moses being in the glorious presence of Christ at the transfiguration.

It is reasonable for a child to expect some sort of inheritance from a loving father. There is an inheritance of biological traits from one's biological father. Where the child's biological father continues to care for them, then there is the further inheritance of modelled behaviours and attitudes. In addition, where the father dies before their child then also there is the inheritance of mementoes and assets upon the death of that father. Most fathers would desire to provide an inheritance for their children.

In the period of the New Testament, under Roman law, all the children of a father were equally his inheritors. Paul, as a Roman citizen, would have been aware of this law. So, when writing to "all in Rome who are loved by God" (Romans 1:7), Paul says that "The Spirit himself testifies with our spirit that we are God's children. Now if we are children, then we are heirs —heirs of God and co-heirs with Christ," (Romans 8:16-17a). As God's

---

[4] The Weight of Glory by C.S. Lewis copyright C.S. Lewis Pte. Ltd. 1949. Extract reprinted by permission.

children, and in addition as His heirs, the faithful have the inheritance of ever-lasting life, being in His company with a glorified, renewed, purified spiritual body. The apostle Peter describes this inheritance as "an inheritance that that can never perish, spoil or fade — kept in heaven for you." (1 Peter 1:4).

The apostle John, early in his gospel, writes of God, the Lord Jesus Christ, that "to all who received him, to those who believed in his name, he gave the right to become children of God" (John 1:12). Those who place reliance on God, who trust in Him, receive from Him the status of being His children. Remember that Christ taught His disciples to pray from the status of a child of God, with the words: "Our Father in heaven, hallowed be your name" (Matthew 6:9). Being God's children, these same folk are His heirs.

As an aside, among all the writers of books that form the New Testament canon, Paul most mentions the faithful as inheritors. This is possibly because Paul was writing often to Gentiles who would be subject to Roman law where, as previously mentioned, *all* the children of a father were *equally* his inheritors. By contrast, in Jewish law the first-born male received twice as much as each of the other male children. In Jewish culture, inheritance was of particular self-interest to the male first-born whereas under Roman law all children similarly benefitted as inheritors.

Seventhly, glorification entails work without duress, tiresomeness, conflict or negativity. Indolence or perpetual inactivity is not a characteristic of heaven. Heaven is not a place where folk persistently recline on fluffy clouds.

God works. We in His image also work. To form all we currently call the earth and the heavens, God worked and His work was full of goodness (Genesis 1:31). In Eden, before humanity's disobedience, part of people's purpose also was to work, without negativity, and care for the earth: "The LORD God took the man and put him in the Garden of Eden to *work* it and take care of it." (Genesis 2:15).

Yet a ramification of humanity's disobedience was that the work of any person, invariably at some stage, in some way, became affected by weariness, frustration, and gnawing negativity. "Cursed is the ground because of you; through painful toil you will eat of it all the days of your life. It will produce thorns and thistles for you, and you will eat the plants of the field. By the sweat of your brow you will eat your food until you return to the ground," (Genesis 3:17b-19a).

Initially, before disobedience, work contained no negativity, no tiresomeness. Work was a core activity of God. Christ said, "My Father is always at his *work* to this very day, and I, too, am *working*." (John 5:17). He also said, "My food is to do the will of him who sent me and to finish his *work*." Christ was both a servant and a worker. If we are to be like Him then we also need to serve and work to honour God. The apostle James curtly states, "faith without deeds is dead." (James 2:26). In short, an expression of true faith are works. Christ described Himself as "working" (John 5:17). To be like Him is also to be working, through obedience to Him, doing His will and requesting that His will be done. (Matthew 6:10).

The apostle John also recollected the words of Christ "By this everyone will know that you are my disciples, if you love one another." (John 13:35). To express love involves actions or deeds. These are the works or the outworking of love.

Work that does not honour God, work that involves no response to Him is ultimately inglorious for it does not lead a person into His glorious presence. The Psalmist wisely remarks, "Unless the Lord builds the house, its builders labour in vain. Unless the Lord keeps watch over the city, the watchman stands guard in vain. In vain you rise early and go late to rest, toiling for the bread you eat; He supplies the need of those he loves." (Psalm 127:1-2).

Our work and service, the product of true faith (i.e. reclining a confidence in God that comes from an enabled exposure to His speaking) extends into heaven, for in Revelation 22:3 and in Revelation 7:15 is the mention of those in heaven who constantly serve God and see His face. However, unlike the work and service on earth that is wearying, sometimes painful and marred, there is no weariness, no tearful endeavour in heaven.

On earth, many people grow into old age and lose much of their physical and mental agility and ability to work. Moreover, increasingly as people enter old age they are less capable of being active participants in the lives of others around them, including their families. They are more likely to be observers, sometimes from afar, rather than frequent contributors. Old age is often associated with a shrinking circle of influence and interaction. The decline in activity and ability changes family dynamics with the aged increasingly being reliant on those who are younger. The aged become the onlookers. Hence, the question arises: when we gradually are stripped of human abilities, our physical and mental prowess, how can we be God's worker? Fortunately, we are not solely flesh. We are also spirit and so much of our work becomes the service of prayer or the relaying of praise, concerns and advice as an experienced observer. This can often be unseen spiritual work rather than bodily endeavour and physical utility.

Some readers, at this point will say, "but doesn't the bible say of heaven "They will rest from their labor" (Revelation 14:13)". By way of reply, I share the comments of Albert Barnes (1962) on that verse.

> "The word rendered here "labor" - κόπος - means properly "wailing, grief," from κόπτω, "to beat," and hence, a beating of the breast as in grief. Then the word denotes "toil, labor, effort," John 4:38; 1 Corinthians 3:8; 1 Corinthians 15:58; 2 Corinthians 6:5; 2 Corinthians 10:15; 2 Corinthians 11:23, 2 Corinthians 11:27. It is used here in the sense of wearisome toil in doing good, in promoting religion, in saving souls, in defending the truth. From such toils the redeemed in heaven will be released; for although there will be employment there, it will be without the sense of fatigue or weariness." (p. 1678)

Our labour that constitutes our actions, motivations and attitudes; all these matter to God. He is the judge of our labour (Revelation 22:12) and its true motivation. Yet our actions, motivations and attitudes that constitute our works are not our entrance ticket to glorification, to be in heavenly company. Revelation 14:13 stated fully is, "Then I heard a voice from heaven saying to me, "Write: 'Blessed are the dead who die in the Lord from now on.'" "Yes," says the Spirit, "that they may rest from their labors, and their works follow them.""" (NKJV). Three points are worth emphasising, regarding the final phrases of this verse:

> (i) as previously mentioned, a reward for the faithful is that they can rest from any weariness or drudgery associated with their labour or deeds.

(ii) a person's works (deeds or actions) do not go before them to procure their admittance into God's presence. Rather they follow them after admission, as evidence or indicators of the expression of God's gift of faith in their lives. For remember, "*he* saved us, not because of righteous things we had done, but because of his mercy," (Titus 3:5). God's saving act and His gift of faith should lead to faithful behaviour, visible works or acts illustrative of being faithful (James 2:26). It is the purity of those works, which are the expression of His will, which carries into His presence.

The actions of the faithful that arise from a pure desire to serve Him are not shunned or excluded from heaven. "Nothing impure will ever enter it" (Revelation 21:27). Moreover, actions like faithful prayer already have a place in heaven —"The smoke of the incense, together with the prayers of God's people, went up before God from the angel's hand." (Revelation 8:4).

(iii) the rewards or the consequences of their works follow them into heaven, as God is judge of all we have done (Revelation 22:12). Albert Barnes comments on the last phrase of Revelation 14:13, saying that a person "can take with him none of his gold, his lands, his raiment; none of the honors of this life; none of the means of sensual gratification. All that will go with him will be his character, and the results of his conduct here, and, in this respect, eternity will be but a prolongation of the present life".

Eighthly, glorification is not only the welcoming of our purified persons, but the welcoming of those purified gifts or abilities that often underpin our earthly glory and splendour. Those purified gifts and abilities are part of our purified person. I stress the adjective purified, for Revelation 21:27 states plainly about heaven that "Nothing impure will ever enter it."

At the transfiguration, Moses and Elijah were able to hear, understand, empathise and speak. There was no mental dysfunction, no impaired hearing, no weariness, no anxiety or restlessness, no acrimony, and no slowness or incapacity to speak or comprehend. Moses and Elijah had physical and mental abilities, now unimpaired and purified that continued after death into heaven, into Christ's presence.

Another illustration of life after death is the behaviour of Christ after His resurrection. He interacted with a range of followers. He was able to walk, talk, listen, eat, teach, empathise and lead (Luke 24:36-51; John 20:19-31; John 21:1-14). Whether all these activities and abilities continue into heaven is not clear. To the extent that those gifts or abilities form part of a purified person, then those gifts or abilities are brought into heaven for they are part of the glory and honour of the nations brought into heaven (Revelation 21:26).

The need for purification of our gifts and abilities can be illustrated by examining speech. Each reader will know from their own experience and observations that speech can be used for good or ill. Using speech, we can deceive, be dishonest, be unfair, abusive, be disrespectful and mean. By contrast, we also can use speech to support, encourage, praise, to be fair, kind and honest. It is the purified ability to speak, a work of God that makes us, including our speech, fit for heaven.

Revelation 21:24 says of heaven, "the kings of the earth will bring their splendour into it." In this verse, the Greek word δόξαν (doxan) is translated most often as splendour or glory. Then, Revelation 21:26 also says of heaven, "The glory and honor of the nations will be brought into it." The same Greek word δόξαν (doxan) in this verse is translated almost always as glory. Yet there is debate among commentators as to what is meant by the phrase "glory and honor" or "splendour" (in verse 24) and questions are raised about who are "the nations" in verse 26.

Albert Barnes remarks about Revelation 21:24, "And the kings of the earth do bring their glory and honour into it - All that they consider as constituting their glory, treasures, crowns, scepters, robes. The idea is that all these will be devoted to God in the future days of the church in its glory, and will be, as it were, brought and laid down at the feet of the Saviour in heaven. The language is derived, doubtless, from the description in Isaiah 60:3-14."

Then the commentator Gill says of Revelation 21:26, "The glory of the nations are the people of God, who, though they are reckoned the filth of the world, are the excellent in the earth; these will be brought into this city, and be presented to the King of it, in a glorious manner." Many other commentators agree that "nations" refers to the people of God but also highlight that "nations" especially includes Gentiles from every era and region. Some commentators then additionally ask; what is their "glory"? In essence, for those judged part of God's family, what is the glory they bring into heaven?

It is God's reflected glory. Humanity is God's creation and as Genesis 1:31 says, "God saw all that He had made and it was very good." Moreover, as previously stated, the Psalmist notes, "I praise you because I am fearfully and wonderfully made; your works are wonderful." (Psalm 139:14). We are God's creation; and as such contain and reflect His goodness and wonder. Many things mark out our wonder and marvelousness. Our ability to listen, understand, inquire, empathise, care, teach, speak, help, lead, innovate, entertain or communicate through music, art, film, story-telling, design, physical and mental skill and endeavour. Some of these purified gifts, traits or abilities, reflective of God's glory, will be brought into heaven to honour Him. These things are part of the marvel of God's creation or "The glory and honor of the nations" that "will be brought into" heaven.

Note that God's glory is not enlarged by the nations' glory, because the source of that glory is God. We, the nations, in our purified nature, with manifold abilities, merely reflect the glory that God already has, will have and has expressed already in us.

Reflections on Glorification

The Reliability of Glorification

The first and important point to highlight is that there is already evidence of glorification. Three witnesses, Peter, John and James, record Moses and Elijah as being glorified in the company of the glorified Christ. Luke comments how the appearance of Christ's face changed and how His clothes became as bright as a flash of lightning. Also, Moses and Elijah "appeared in glorious splendour, talking with Jesus" (Luke 9: 31). Here is evidence of people long gone from the earth (i.e. Moses and Elijah) now appearing glorious in the company of a glorious Christ.

Contrast that with those people, down through the ages to the current time, who say there is no heaven; no after-life. They contend that earthly life is all that is on offer to any person. There is no other life, no eternal life. Yet the disciples learned and saw first-hand that a life beyond the grave is possible. Later they saw and experienced for themselves a resurrected Christ. If these events were not real, then a masterful illusionist had cleverly tricked them all. But remember, the disciples had been in the constant company of Christ for a couple of years; ample time to discern if Jesus Christ was a skilled illusionist or if He was liable to willingly participate in such illusion. The disciples had ample time to discern if He could be trusted, if He was deceitful or masterful at trickery. These disciples had seen much that was unusual, miraculous; yet always their judgement was that these events were real, as was the judgement of others who participated in or observed those events. The disciples were confident in their veracity. Yet even when one of the disciples, namely Thomas, doubted that the

Christ was real, Christ gave him opportunity to see and feel his purified wounds so that by touching and seeing Thomas could gain the assurance that Christ, who died, was risen anew (John 20:24-27). The glorification of Christ in the glorified company of Moses and Elijah and the viewing of the wounds in the risen Christ were instances to add to their list of things they had witnessed that were remarkable and unique.

Hence, bluntly, as we each approach our deaths we can reflect on this evidence, this testimony of James, Peter and John, that life after death on earth is possible. John's words about Christ are worth pausing to consider. This is the same disciple who was one of the witnesses of the transfiguration and much else. John says, "For God so loved the world that He gave His one and only Son, that everyone who believes in Him shall not perish but have *eternal life*. For God did not send His Son into the world to condemn the world, but to save the world through Him." (John 3:16-17). This same John also remembered some other related comments of Christ — "Do not let your hearts be troubled. You believe in God; believe in Me as well. In My Father's house are many rooms. If it were not so, would I have told you that I am going there to prepare a place for you? And if I go and prepare a place for you, I will come back and welcome you into My presence, so that *you also may be where I am*." (John 14:1-3). The three disciples had already seen two long dead servants of God, Moses and Elijah, be alive where Christ was.

Besides witnesses of glorification providing evidence for glorification, there is also the evidence of the trustworthiness of what God says and what his servants say. The Psalmist says of God "The statutes you have laid down are righteous; they are fully trustworthy." (Psalm 119: 138). There are around 80 verses where Christ is quoted specifically by the gospel writers to say, "I tell you the truth."

Importantly, when the disciple Thomas asks Christ, "Lord, we don't know where you are going, so how can we know the way?" (John 14:5); Christ answers by saying; "I am the way and the *truth* and the life. No one comes to the Father except through me." (John 14:6). Christ names Himself as the truth; that which is utterly reliable, trustworthy, unsullied and accurate. Years after Christ's death and resurrection, God commands the apostle John, when writing the Book of Revelation, "Write this down, for these words are trustworthy and true." (Revelation 21: 5).

In Eden, it was the truthfulness of God's word that Satan questioned and refuted. Eve correctly remembered God's words; "God did say, 'You must not eat fruit from the tree that is in the middle of the garden, and you must not touch it, or you will surely die.'" (Genesis 3:3). However, Satan lied to Eve and in so doing attacked the trustworthiness of God's words by saying, "You will not surely die." (Genesis 3:4).

If God's word is trustworthy then so are His promises. Hence, the promises to Eve (Genesis 3:15) and the Jewish people down through the subsequent centuries that a redeemer, a saviour and messiah would be sent by God were promises God would uphold. The most unambiguous proof that Jesus Christ was the fulfilment of God's promise to the Jewish people, and all humanity, was His resurrection. The miracles, the transfiguration, the voices from heaven that said, "This is my Son" (Matthew 3:17, Luke 9:35) were additional indicators of His power and status. His power over death, His resurrection, however, uniquely marked Him out. As Paul said: "if Christ has not been raised, your faith is futile; you are still in your sins." (1 Corinthians 15:17).

So when Christ speaks of heaven saying, "My Father's house has many rooms; if that were not so, would I have told you that I am going there to prepare a place for you? And if I go and prepare a place for you, I will come back and take you to be with me that you also may be where I am." (John 14:2,3) there is much evidence pointing to His statement being truthful. On another occasion, He says, "I say to you that many will come from the east and the west, and will take their places at the feast with Abraham, Isaac and Jacob in the kingdom of heaven." (Matthew 8:11). Not only is Christ commenting on the veracity of heaven but also that God's servants, like Abraham, Isaac and Jacob, will be in heaven and heaven will contain a multitude of people across the globe from many ages. Moreover, even in heaven, Abraham, Isaac and Jacob still will be recognisable.

Paul was unlike the disciples. Like us, Paul did not walk with Jesus Christ in Galilee and its surrounds. Paul had no first-hand knowledge of all the events associated with that walk, the miracles and the audible voices from heaven. Nonetheless, Paul came to the same conviction as the disciples and other witnesses that Jesus was raised from the dead and was the messiah and Son of God. This is made clear in his letter to the Philippians where he writes of Christ Jesus being in very nature God

(Philippians 2:5). Yet for many years in Paul's adult life, this was not his view of Christ. He actively persecuted followers of Christ, assessing them to be miscreants and perverters of the Law. It is likely that when told by followers of the Way that Christ was resurrected, and that He had been seen subsequently by hundreds, Paul would have dismissed their statements as lies or apparitions, the consequences of acute grief. Their statements alone were not persuasive to Paul. Yet it needs to be noted that years later, in one of his letters, Paul would say that the views and statements of these many people existed and, by inference, were complementary evidence of his personal view and experience of the resurrected Christ (Acts 9:3-6).

Paul's confidence in Christ was not the simple product of reliance on the views of these scores of witnesses. Rather it stemmed from accumulated personal experiences and knowledge of the work of Christ. It did not solely start with his blinding interaction with Christ on the road to Damascus (Acts 9:3-6) but, far earlier, in learning the Law and later hearing the witness of the people of the Way who spoke plainly or even under duress about what they heard Christ say and saw Him do. After his interaction with the risen Christ on the road to Damascus, Paul, when in Arabia, would have grappled with his learned understanding of what the Law and prophets said about the messiah and how that meshed with what he now knew about Jesus Christ. We are not privy to the exact timeline by which Paul came fully to the realisation and confidence that Christ, raised from the dead, was the messiah and Son of God. We do know that he formed a firm, deep-seated understanding of Christ's status and nature that propelled him for the rest of his adult life. His confidences in Christ were fashioned through the accumulation of experiences with Christ and the work of God's Spirit, known also as the Helper, Advocate or Comforter (See John 14:26 amplified bible).

While on earth, Christ gave the disciples the hope of a Comforter and Advocate, the Spirit of God. Christ said, "I will ask the Father, and he will give you another advocate to help you and be with you forever— the Spirit of truth." (John 14:16,17). The naming of the Spirit of God as the 'Spirit of truth' emphasises the trustworthiness and truthfulness of God.

The disciples did not need to live long in hope of receipt of the Spirit. The trustworthiness of Christ's words was verified, for at Pentecost the Spirit filled them. "All of them were filled with the Holy Spirit" (Acts 2:4).

This is yet another example of a hope, an anticipation, an expectation being fulfilled and God's promises being trustworthy.

The trustworthiness of God's words and promises are supported by the work of His Spirit that produces "love, joy, peace, forbearance, kindness, goodness, faithfulness, gentleness, and self-control." (Galatians 5:22,23). God's Spirit pours peace (i.e. assurance) and love into our hearts (Romans 5:5) making real to us that He loves us and so His promises of loving us and His offering the hope of glory does not disappoint. When He promises glorification, because He is truthful and trustworthy, it is a firm hope, something destined to occur. Therefore, a hope in glorification is not forlorn. It is an event simply yet to occur, rather than an incorrect, empty anticipation.

A verse already mentioned, Matthew 5:3, says, "Blessed are the poor in spirit, for theirs is the kingdom of heaven." Note the choice of verb. The writer of Matthew's gospel, in capturing the Aramaic words of Christ, chose deliberately to use the Greek word ἐστιν (i.e. is) rather than ἐσται (i.e. will be) — such that in English we write, "for theirs *is* the kingdom of heaven" rather than writing, "for theirs ***will be*** the kingdom of heaven." This is the certainty of heaven for the person who in God's sight is blessed. In a legal sense, such a person already *is* a citizen of heaven, although in a practical sense is yet to enter heaven. The glory of the kingdom of heaven is a reliable anticipation. Having the legal right to citizenship of heaven is not just a future event. It is a legal status available even now to those still living on the earth. The enjoyment of that legal status, however, comes after our earthly demise.

Perhaps a human analogy may aid clarity. Imagine parents who assign in their will certain assets to one of their children, then that child is the legal inheritor of those assets, provided there is no alteration or challenge to the will and the child outlives their parents. Similarly, when God's assessment of a person is that they are blessed, then that person's legal status *is now* a citizen, an inheritor, of heaven. Their place in heaven may await but their legal claim is already secure.

This present legal underpinning of the glory of heaven is not always given precedence in the scriptures, causing glorification often to be described as a future event, something to anticipate. Nevertheless, the legal underpinning of glorification makes that future event possible. John writes, "what we will be has not yet appeared." (1 John 3:2 ESV). Hence, the act of glorification is an expectation, something to hope for rather than to experience presently, immediately.

When Paul writes about hope, he says, "hope does not disappoint us." (Romans 5:5). Why? Why does the expectation or hope in glorification not disappoint? Why is it viewed with such confidence and certainty by Paul and others; rather than being seen or questioned as a potential falsehood? The answer is because of the trustworthiness, the reliability and the power of God who promises the glorification, who intends it, authors it and creates its legal foundation. At heart, it is the reliability and truthfulness of God's word that makes the hope of glorification not forlorn, not a legal or emotional falsehood.

One of the sad features of modernity is its widespread ignorance and distrust in the many historical facts that underpin Christianity. This leads to people viewing faith in God as having no factual basis. Faith is not viewed as God's gift, underpinned by reliable real events in history. Rather it is viewed as a wholly subjective act with no sound basis in history. Faith is viewed as wishful, unsubstantiated thinking. It is viewed as irrationality or blind stupidity rather than as a response underpinned by facts.

Understanding glorification can change our perceptions of one another

The second reflection on glorification is a corollary of the first and, for me, comes from reading C.S. Lewis's sermon given in June 1941, during the darkness of World War II, when Lewis spoke at the Church of St Mary in Oxford. Macmillan later published the sermon under the title "Weight of Glory" in 1949.

The nub of Lewis's sermon can be summarised by first observing that glorification (being glorified) is God's loving gift to those who have faith in Him (i.e. genuinely honouring Him, being truly devoted to Him). Magnetic to our gaze and mind might be the rich images of glorification, especially as portrayed in religious paintings, yet nonetheless Lewis turned the minds of his listeners (and later his readers when the sermon was published) towards their neighbours. He wrote a remarkably powerful insight about glorification when he said of a believer:

> "It may be possible to think too much of his (*i.e. the believer's*) own potential glory hereafter; it is hardly possible for him to think too often or too deeply about that of his neighbour. The load, or weight, or burden of my neighbour's glory should be laid daily on my back, a load so heavy that only humility can carry it, and the backs of the proud will be broken. It is a serious thing to live in a society of possible gods and goddesses, to remember that the dullest and most uninteresting person you talk to may one day be a creature which, if you saw it now, you would be strongly tempted to worship, or else a horror and a corruption such as you now meet, if at all, only in a nightmare. All day long we are, in some degree, helping each other to one or other of these destinations......There are no ordinary people. You have never talked to a mere mortal." (pages 14-15, in "The Weight of Glory", C.S. Lewis, W.B. Eerdmans Publishing Company, Grand Rapids, Michigan, USA, 1965).[5]

Is not the potential glory of our neighbour, the casual acquaintance, the work colleague and those we serve, a cause for prayer? Saint Paul encourages those at Philippi to "bring up all your requests to God in your prayers and petitions, along with giving thanks." (Philippians 4:6). Is it not apt to give thanks to God each day for those around us, for they are part of the table God prepares for us (Psalm 23:5)? Is it not proper to petition God to lead into His presence those with whom we interact? Moreover, should we not simultaneously give thanks to Him and for the work of His only Son, the Lord Jesus Christ, who makes that journey possible for any person, and His Spirit that empowers such persons on that journey? Understanding the journey to glorification changes our perceptions of one another and helps beneficially change our responses to one another. It leads to thanksgiving.

In a similar vein it is worth reflecting on the fact that the risen Christ

---

[5] The Weight of Glory by C.S. Lewis copyright C.S. Lewis Pte. Ltd. 1949. Extract reprinted by permission.

was recognizable to His disciples by His actions (John 21: 5-12), in the way he broke bread (Luke 24: 30,31), and by His general appearance (Matthew 28: 17). He was no stranger. The same is likely for us. In heaven, somehow we will be recognizable to those known to us while we lived on the earth. If these folk can recognise us in Heaven, then should we not recognise them while we reside on earth? Should we not recognise and care for those around us while on the earth. Among those are His folk and He is in His folk as evidenced by Him saying:

> "For I was hungry and you gave me something to eat, I was thirsty and you gave me something to drink, I was a stranger and you invited me in. I needed clothes and you clothed me, I was sick and you looked after me, I was in prison and you came to visit me. Then the righteous will answer him, 'Lord, when did we see you hungry and feed you, or thirsty and give you something to drink?' When did we see you a stranger and invite you in, or needing clothes and clothe you? When did we see you sick or in prison and go to visit you?' The King will reply, 'Truly I tell you, whatever you did for one of the least of these brothers and sisters of mine, you did for me.'" (Matthew 25:35-40)

Note our care, at best at core, is motivated by His first and on-going love for us. His love flows into us and through us to those around us. Our loving actions start from His love for us, then poured out to others. "Unless the LORD builds the house, the builders labor in vain. Unless the LORD watches over the city, the guards stand watch in vain." (Psalm 127:1).

Glorification is a status and an outcome

Often in paintings, glorification is displayed as emanating rays of vivid light. Yet C.S. Lewis found nothing particularly appealing about the prospect of such luminosity. In his published sermon, mentioned previously, he wrote, "Who wishes to become a kind of living electric light bulb?" Yet glory is more than conspicuous clarity that bright light provides;

it is also a status and an outcome. The status and outcome is being in the company of Christ, for Colossians 3:4 states: "When Christ, who is your life, appears, then you also will appear with him in glory."

Glorification signals and results from the status of being judged and recognised as a child of God. The apostle Paul plainly states: "You are all sons of God through faith in Christ Jesus," (Galatians 3:26). Elsewhere he quotes Old Testament verses describing God speaking "'I will be a Father to you, and you will be my sons and daughters,' says the Lord Almighty." (2 Corinthians 6:18).

Regarding the phrase "children of God", Martyn Lloyd-Jones noted that the more he read the New Testament, the more he was impressed by the fact that every appeal for conduct and good living and behaviour made in the New Testament was always made in terms of a person's position or status. He observed that godly conduct rested on a person's understanding of their status as a child of God. Through the gift of faith in Jesus Christ, believers or followers of Christ receive the status of children of God. That status qualifies them to be welcomed by God into His heavenly home for He is their loving Father.

C.S. Lewis soberly explores having a status that qualifies one to be in the company of Christ in heaven. Drawing on the scriptures, he notes that in the end God's face will turn to gaze on each of us and with that look will confer either glory inexpressible, or a shame that can never be cured or disguised. He notes how scripture indicates that we shall all stand before God and we each shall be inspected and judged. Importantly and succinctly, Lewis comments that:

> "The promise of glory is the promise, almost incredible and only possible by the work of Christ, that some of us, that any of us who really chooses, shall actually survive that examination, shall find approval, shall please God. To please God....to be a real ingredient in the divine happiness....to be loved by God, not merely pitied, but delighted in as an artist delights in his work or a father in a son---it seems impossible,

a weight or burden of glory which our thoughts can hardly sustain. But so it is." (ibid, p. 10)[6]

Glorification (being glorified) as a status and outcome is also highlighted by other great Christian minds and scholars. By illustration, Alexander MacLaren (1904), a famous English Baptist minister, said:

> "The highest end, the great purpose of the Gospel and of all God's dealings with us in Christ Jesus is to make us like our Lord. As we have borne the image of the earthly we shall also bear the image of the heavenly. 'We, beholding the glory, are changed into the glory.'"

As evidenced by the behaviour of Moses and Elijah, after their death and subsequent glorification made visible during the transfiguration (Matthew 17:1–8, Mark 9:2–8, Luke 9:28–36 and 2 Peter 1:16–18), there can be great comfort and euphony in the presence of the glorified Christ.

The journey to glorification is via purification and via our exposure to Him, and the resultant exposure of our true selves. I explore this statement using the illustration of the apostle Peter (Luke 4:31-5:11). This long passage describes how firstly Christ made it possible, and at other times inevitable, that what He did and said would be noticed by Peter. Thus, Peter had many opportunities to observe and assess the person of Christ, long before Peter was ever a willing disciple of Christ. Peter observed and was exposed to Christ as teacher and healer. In addition, Peter saw Christ in small groups, or amid crowds or being alone. Peter saw Him eat and engage in home life. He saw Him in the formal setting of the synagogue and the informality of the field. Peter saw Him attend to and heal his mother-in-law.

According to biblical scholarship, it is likely that Peter and his bother Andrew grew up in Bethsaida (John 1:44), a town on the northern shores of the Sea of Galilee. Bethsaida is an Aramaic word meaning 'house of fishing' or 'fisherman's house'. Peter and Andrew's father was a fisherman and, as was common practice, the sons entered the same livelihood. Bethsaida lay just inside the region known as Gaulanitis and was a town

---

[6] The Weight of Glory by C.S. Lewis copyright C.S. Lewis Pte. Ltd. 1949. Extract reprinted by permission.

with Greek and Jewish influences. Andrew's name, for example, is Greek and means 'manly'. Jews and Gentiles would have resided in Bethsaida, so Peter and Andrew would have seen and interacted with Gentiles. Peter, Andrew and their family appear to have moved to Capernaum (Mark 1:21, 29-31) or perhaps they also had a home in Capernaum as Bethsaida and Capernaum were only about 7 kilometres apart.

Bethsaida and Capernaum were nearby the shore of the Sea of Galilee, a large inland freshwater body about 22 kilometres, north to south, and about 13 kilometres across. The commerce of both towns centred on fishing. The ancient Jewish historian Josephus states that there were more than 230 fishing boats working on the Sea of Galilee during this period of Jewish history. A typical fishing boat was about seven metres long and just over two metres, with a crew four rowers plus another to steer and supervise the catch. Fishing was not without is dangers as storms could quickly develop over the Sea of Galilee (Matthew 8: 23–27).

A boat could carry a half tonne of fish and the nets carried in the boats were made of flax or linen, with most fishing occurring at night when fish would less easily see and swim around the nets. In deep water fishing, two or three boats would work together to set up a net between them and chase fish into the net. This action would be repeated seven or eight times during the night. Near daybreak, the fishermen would bring in their catch. They would sort the catch for sale, wash the nets to remove debris and silt, then mend and dry the nets ready for the next day's catch.

Hence, it is not unusual that one of the occasions, when Peter is exposed to Christ, involves Jesus standing on the shores of the lake speaking to people as they crowded around Him. Jesus noticed two fishing boats near the lake's shore, left there while the fishermen washed their nets. He climbed into one of the boats, one belonging to Peter, and as He already knew Peter, He asked Peter to push his boat out a little, which also indicated that Peter was within earshot and therefore Peter probably overheard the subsequent teaching of Jesus. Jesus sat in Peter's boat and from there taught the people. When He finished speaking to those who had gathered, He asked Peter to put out into the deep water and let down the nets for a catch.

What Jesus was asking of Peter was not a small thing. Firstly, Peter, his crew and fellow fishermen in the other boats were tired, as Peter intimated.

It was now daytime and they already had fished all night, without success. Christ's request meant that Peter, as the master of the boat, would need to ask his tired crew, and the other supporting boat, firstly to load the nets into the boats, secondly, arduously row out to reach deep water and then finally, lower their nets in the hope for a catch, at a time of day when fishing was already known to be likely less successful. With great respect for Jesus, Peter calls Him, Ἐπιστάτα (Epistata) which can be translated as master, teacher or chief. "Master, we've worked hard all night and haven't caught anything. But because you say so, I will let down the nets." (Luke 5:5).

Importantly, after rowing out and catching such a vast haul of fish that their nets began to fray, and the boats were sinking under the weight of the fish, Peter realises that more than a lesson in fishing was at play here. Peter calls Jesus by a new name, Κύριε (Kyrie) which translates as lord, master, sir or the Lord. In recording the interchange between Peter and Jesus, Luke uses two different words to describe the change in status of Christ in Peter's perception; first Epistata then Kyrie, or first master then Lord.

Luke, when writing of the incident, up to this point has always named Peter as Simon; but then signals the change at work within Peter by calling him for the very first time Simon Peter. The outcome of Jesus' exposure to Peter has led Peter to a judgement that Jesus was the Lord. A ramification was that Peter, by comparison, assessed himself as "I am a sinful man." (Luke 5:8). So different was Peter's assessment of himself relative to Christ that Peter wished Christ to depart from his presence. Why this reaction?

Previously and often, when Christ created bounty, such as turning water into wine or removing sickness or affliction, the reaction He received was praise, thanksgiving and wonder. Yet here the bounty of fish generates a desire for separation. Peter requests: "Go away from me, Lord; I am a sinful man!" (Luke 5:8).

I consider that Peter at this point, after seeing first-hand yet another example of the bounty of Christ with all the power, authority and generosity that entailed, recognised Christ as utterly blessed by God; uniquely pure and powerful. By comparison, Peter was belittled, flawed and ordinary. Peter falls to his knees when addressing Christ, physically symbolising his status before Christ.

Christ exercised power, and was pure-hearted. He cared for these fishermen who had toiled for hours the previous night and caught nothing, which meant no money from fish sales, or fish to eat from their catch, for them or their families. In contrast to the power, generosity and kindness of Christ, Peter knew himself to be simply sinful, impure and limited. In Peter's mind, someone so pure and powerful like Christ needed to be kept separate from someone like Peter who was a sinful man. As a Jew, familiar with Mosaic law, Peter would know the need to remove impurity. What was holy needed to be kept separate and apart from all that could defile.

He, as a sinful man, was a source of corruption and defilement and was unworthy to be in the company of one as pure, holy and powerful as the Christ, the Lord. The immensity of the catch of fish was but one more confirmation that Christ was what his brother Andrew had told Peter — Christ was the messiah, the One of whom the disciple Philip later said, "We have found the one Moses wrote about in the Law, and about whom the prophets also wrote — Jesus of Nazareth, the son of Joseph." (John 1:45). It was Andrew who earlier had said to Peter, his brother, about Jesus; "We have found the Messiah" (i.e., the Christ) (John 1:41).

Peter's reflection on his inner person was that he was unworthy to be in Christ's company. He also knew he was unlike his mother-in-law or the many others with illnesses or afflictions he had seen or heard about who experienced the power and empathy of Christ. Peter did not share their physical or mental ailments. By contrast, Peter was physically strong, capable and commercially industrious. His issue was not his physical or mental lack to be in need of Christ's healing care. Rather, Peter's ailment was a spiritual lack. He was marred by sin and could only be a contaminant of Christ. Christ needed to be placed away from him, not near him.

I cannot find the words to express how devastating, how raw and discomforting it is to know that at core one is unfit for heaven, ruined and stained by sin; and to be ashamed and without excuse before God.

That awareness and its valley of suffering is a necessary part of the path to heaven and is a sign that one is on that road. As Christ Himself said:

> "Blessed are the poor in spirit, for theirs is the kingdom
> of heaven.
> Blessed are those who mourn, for they will be comforted."
> (Matthew 5:3,4)

Those made aware of their spiritual poverty, their being stained and lessened by sin (Isaiah 6:5) and their need of Him have the promise of sharing with Him in the wonder, the safety and freedom of heaven. They will be comforted (Isaiah 6:7), made new and not left exposed. They will not be corroded by want. Alternatively, said in reverse, those blessed by God are those whose resultant inner awareness includes an illumination of their poverty of spirit before God.

As an aside, in the sermon on the mount Christ outlines what it means to be blessed (Matthew 5:3-12), including the statements in Matthew 5:3,4 quoted above. Now, however, by the lakeside He models what He will later say on the mount through his actions and words to Peter. By the lakeside, in the company of Christ, Peter becomes aware of his spiritual poverty by being surrounded by the purity and power of Christ (I would like to say that the Spirit of God makes possible that awareness in Peter of his spiritual poverty). What Christ says to Peter by the lakeside comforts him. Hence, when Christ, later on the mount, makes His statements about what it is to be blessed, Peter is aware of the veracity of these statements because he has already experienced this comfort in his lakeside interaction with Christ. Peter has experienced the rawness of his sinful self; yet also experienced the freeing and comforting words and actions of Christ.

Much later, when Peter thrice denies knowledge of Christ (Matthew 26:69-75; John 18:15-27; Luke 22:54-62); once again Peter, in remembering the words of Christ (Matthew 26:75), becomes aware of his great poverty of spirit. He 'wept bitterly' (Matthew 26:75; Luke 22:62). The Greek word *pikrós*, that we translate as bitterly, also conveys the notion of piercing and violence. Peter's sobbing was violent and piercing. It shook him to his core. Yet in its aftermath, Peter was able to remember Christ's prayer for him: "Simon, Simon, Satan has asked to sift you as wheat. But I have prayed for you, Simon, that your faith may not fail. And when you have turned back, strengthen your brothers." (Luke 22:31).

Christ gave Peter both an anticipation of his denial but also knowledge of His care for Peter and His desire that Peter should turn once more towards Him and then care for those around him. Again, this is Christ acting out what He said in the Beatitudes that those who were blessed were those comforted and welcomed into heaven via a journey of being enabled to perceive their spiritual poverty and then mourn their lack. Christ's prayers and actions were the source of Peter's eventual comforting, when he once again, by denying his association with Christ, then became aware of his spiritual poverty and yet remembered Christ's deep care for him and that was his comfort; being loved by Christ.

At the lakeside, when Christ replies to Peter, Christ does not dispute Peter's assessment of himself or Jesus. He accepts those assessments but He also does not leave Peter. Instead, He answers Peter's fear of being a contaminant with his irksome awareness of being unworthy to be in Christ's presence. Christ first says, "Fear not". In this phrase, the Greek word φοβέομαι (*phobeó*) that is translated as fear means to put to flight, to terrify or frighten. Peter was fearful of corrupting Christ, of being unworthy, with distance needing to be placed between himself and Christ; of him not deserving in any way to be in the presence of Christ.

Importantly, Christ then gives Peter a reason not to be fearful, not to consider distancing himself from Christ. He says words to Peter that Peter finds comforting, so enabling and powerful, that Peter immediately is able to follow Christ. Christ says to Peter "from now on you will catch men", (Luke 5:10). The writer of Matthew's gospel also makes clear that Christ's invitation was extended to Peter's brother, Andrew: "Come, follow me and I will make you fishers of men." (Matthew 4:19).

If Christ had instructed me to be a "fisher of men" then I suspect my reaction would have been the opposite of Peter's and more aligned to Moses' response, being full of hesitancy (Exodus 3:11). For reasons I am not much aware of, Peter found Christ's invitation seemingly easy to accept. Peter was not alarmed or perturbed by Christ's offer; neither was Andrew. Both willingly left their task of fishing. As was the case with their fellow fishermen, James and John, their task of fishing was passed to their hired hands (Mark 1:20) whilst they travelled in the company of Jesus. Christ's offer that they all would no longer be immersed in the commerce of fishing but rather would be interacting with people, not fish, was greatly attractive to them. The Greek word for "catch" in the phrase "from now on you will catch men" means "to catch alive" or to capture for life. Peter and Andrew appeared freed and invigorated by accepting Christ's invitation.

Exactly what Christ's call to Peter and Andrew meant to them is difficult to gauge. Certainly, from our point in history it is clear that later the disciples would cast the net of God's gospel, and many people would be drawn up from their depths of sin and alienation from God into salvation and sanctification. However, in the language and thinking of Peter and Andrew at that time by the lakeside, it is not exactly clear to me why they viewed Christ's invitation so positively and enticing. Moreover, the attraction to follow Christ was not without cost, for much later, as a disciple of Jesus and having been in Christ's company for a couple of years, Peter exclaims to Christ "We have left everything to follow you!" (Mark 10: 28).

It may be that a key part of the captivation of Christ's invitation was the chance to participate in the work of the messiah. Andrew, Peter's brother, had already formed the view that Jesus was the messiah (John 1:41). Both Peter and Andrew would have been sufficiently well versed in the writings of the Old Testament to know the messiah would come with power and authority and would be from David's line. Importantly, the common view at that time was that the messiah would free the Jewish people from the servitude of Roman occupation. Hence, it may be that Christ's invitation was viewed through the political lens of freeing people from Roman domination. To be a participant in such a grand venture, with all the accolades that would surround it, could well have been enticing. Certainly, the later behaviour of these disciples reveals that they were attracted by status and honour. Mark 9:34, Luke 9:46, Mark 10:41 and Luke 22:24 all outline dispute and argument among the disciples about who among them was the greatest.

Why have I spent so long re-telling this interaction between Christ and Peter? Simply to show that Peter's journey into heavenly glorification, where he would be made anew, purified and made acceptable to God, to be judged as one redeemed by Christ, judged to be a child of God, was first via his being exposed to Christ and more importantly, vice versa.

We, like Peter face a journey to glorification via purification and via our exposure to Him and the exposure of our true selves. Being exposed to Christ and His inestimable persistent care for us reveals our unsightly core and our need to be covered by His righteousness, His saving act and grace. Glorification follows from time in His company. The duration of that time can range from being momentary or for much of a long lifetime. Ultimately, believers in Christ receive from Him a gift only He can give for He says in prayer to His Father "I have given them the glory that you gave me, that they may be one as we are one." (John 17:22). Christ's glory is His acceptability with God, His purity. Christ's saving act, God's gospel, is His gift to us that ensures we can receive the status of acceptability with God. This is our ultimate glory, having acceptance with God, being allowed and enabled to participate in the thrill of heaven. C.S. Lewis describes this as ultimately having fame with God.

Glory and glorification are portrayed as a winsome brilliance, a power, a purity and confident clarity; yet it is easy to lose sight of their pathway being via our exposure to Him. This can be as brief as the interchange near death between the criminal and Christ, when the offender, after recognising that Christ had done no wrong, says to Christ; "Jesus, remember me when you come into your kingdom." Christ replies, "I tell you the truth, today you will be with me in paradise." (Luke 23:41-43). For most people, however, exposure to Christ, and vice versa, occurs over a longer timeframe and the journey to glorification is far longer; not in a single day. Glorification is an outcome of our interaction with God and being glorified is a status and gift due to God's saving act, His gospel.

The last line in the last verse of the often sung Christmas carol "Away in a Manger" reminds us how God makes us fit be to in His company in heaven. The entire last verse is:

> "Be near me Lord Jesus I ask you to stay
> Close by me for ever, and love me, I pray.
> Bless all the dear children in Your tender care,
> And fit us for heaven, to live with You there." (Kirkpatrick 1895)

Glorification involves no negativity

Being glorified is to be made fit to be in God's presence; being made able and capable to serve Him, without impediment (Revelation 22:3, Revelation 7:15). While on earth, we face many impediments. Our flesh limits us. We face appetites within and around us that so easily lead us away from serving Him and being receptive to His leading. Even our seemingly best efforts often are tinged with negativity.

We offer time and energy in prayer, study or helping others; at expense of time with our families or friends. There is often a real cost, a penalty we carry or impose on others, even when sure of the justness of our actions. Ever since Eden when the bounty of Nature became tinged with the toil over weeds, thorns and difficulty; such has remained our lot. In all earth-bound activity is the abrasion and bruising of some form of negativity. We may be "wonderfully made" but not all our actions, reactions, thoughts and words are wonderful. Negativity lurks in all corners, in various forms and degrees.

Yet in the purity of heaven, there is no corrosive, debilitating negativity. It is His domain which is why in the Lord's prayer we say "Thy will be done on earth as it is in heaven." Heaven is where His will is exercised; where the negativity and stain of sin is removed. Yet on earth where we have withdrawn, as a people, our trust and obedience to Him; the daily consequence is endeavour amid thorn and weed. By contrast, there is no such negativity in glorification.

According to Meyer (1898), there is an old story of some monks to whom the Book of Revelation was being read. At the end of the reading, each monk was asked to reveal which promise in the book he most enjoyed. One opted for; "God shall wipe away all tears." Another chose, "To him that overcometh I will give to sit on My throne." A third monk indicated his delight in the promise, "His servants shall serve Him." This third person was Thomas à Kempis who afterward wrote *The Imitation of Christ*, originally written in Latin as *De Imitatione Christi* in the early 15th century. Thomas à Kempis' preference was to be like Christ, to be a servant of God. Unlike the situation on earth, being a servant and worker in heaven involves no weariness, no negativity of boredom, no frustration or fear of failure or inadequacy. There is work in heaven that is pleasant, captivating and engaging with no residue of tiredness, pointlessness or negativity.

In glory is the durability of God's armour

Paul says of the armour God lovingly provides:

> "Put on the full armour of God, so that you can take your stand against the devil's schemes. For our struggle is not against flesh and blood, but against the rulers, against

the authorities, against the powers of this dark world and against the spiritual forces of evil in the heavenly realms. Therefore put on the full armour of God, so that when the day of evil comes, you may be able to stand your ground, and after you have done everything, to stand. Stand firm then, with the belt of truth buckled around your waist, with the breastplate of righteousness in place, and with your feet fitted with the readiness that comes from the gospel of peace. Take the helmet of salvation and the sword of the Spirit, which is the word of God." (Ephesians 6:11-17)

This is the armour of God and therefore, like God, it endures; even into heaven. Take the gift of faith. Paul soberly summarises that "everything that does not come from faith is sin." (Romans 14:23). For the sake of emphasis, I repeat the words: All that does not come from faith is sin. Because God is devoid of sin, it is faith not sin that is acceptable to Him. It follows that faith is durable in the presence of God in whom there is no sin. Hence, acts of faith such as "prayers of the faithful" can rise up before God in heaven and be kept and honoured as fragrant incense (Revelation 5:8). Already in heaven is the purity of faith; by faith are we saved and therefore are made safe in God's presence by that faith. Faith is God's gift, His property, made available to all with ears and heart to receive it. Because it is His gift, His property, it endures in His presence, even in heaven.

Being glorified is to be a participant in and citizen of the "new heavens and new earth" following the Judgment Day (Matthew 6:19-20). Paul wrote that our citizenship is in heaven (Philippians 3:20). He also said that we have one hope, and that our hope is in heaven (Ephesians 4:4; Colossians 1:5). Heaven, where God is, is freedom from sin, death (Revelation 21: 4) and darkness (Revelation 22:5). Faith, enabled reliance on and simple devotion to God, reigns in this eternal home. A property or characteristic of faith is its durability in God's presence, in His glorious presence.

God's armour protects and preserves us. His righteousness, truth, and faith are powerful and lasting. They are His enduring gifts to us, carried into and richly residing in the glory of heaven.

The wait for glorification

Those who place their confidence in Christ have the certainty of glorification in heaven, but also the duty to serve the Lord while they live and wait on the earth. There is a risk, and there are examples in history, where the eager expectation of heaven leads to carelessness and wantonness in people's attitudes and behaviours. There is a need to remember the example of the Lord Jesus while he walked the earth. The sick and incapacitated He healed. The hungry He fed. Those eager to learn He taught. To those in darkness He gave Light. Those in error He rebuked. His life was full of walking, talking, teaching and caring. He was never careless, never wanton; ever prayerful.

Yet it does require saying that even if one's life is full of service, with moments and occasions of great joy, exhilaration and comfort, nonetheless there will also be an underlying restlessness for the great wonder of heaven and His welcome. While one waits for glorification, one need not wait for death to experience God's glory. We may wait for the glory of heaven, but God's glory is already manifest; so in that way we need not wait to experience God's glory.

"But you, LORD, are a shield around me, my glory, the One who lifts my head high." (Psalm 3:3). This was a psalm composed by King David during, or on reflection of, his fleeing from his son Absalom who sought his death. Even near the jaws of death, David knew that the glory that would endure was God's glory. In his commentary on this psalm, Albert Barnes says that David's glory (i.e. "my glory") was that David could unreservedly place his trust in God. It was an honour for David, in this time of danger and trouble, to rely on God. In another famous psalm, David was comforted by his knowledge of God's abiding care. "You prepare a table before me in the presence of my enemies." (Psalm 23:5). This was the glory, the majesty and power of God that would endure from life on earth into the courts of heaven.

While we live on earth, it is worth dwelling on our true purpose. As previously stated: the Westminster Catechism's first question and answer is:

Q: What is the chief end of man?

A: Man's chief end is to glorify God, and to enjoy him forever.

This is a journey we can begin on earth and carry into heaven.

For some, the wait for heaven will be long. Some will grow frail, physically or mentally marred. Minds and limbs will atrophy. Only their withered frame or diminished essence will be their fading presence at death. Yet God, their loving Father, will welcome them, clothing them anew with everlasting purified spiritual bodies fit for heaven, for they have received and exercised His gift of faith and so are recognised in heaven as one of His many children. At death, they may be mentally impaired, even vegetative; yet God honours His promises. God will now welcome these folk, who in earlier years exercised their gift of faith.

For some, at some point in the history of this earth, their wait for glorification will be interrupted by the return of Christ, His second coming. On this occasion, when He comes again in power and glory, "every eye will see Him" (Revelation 1:7). At that glorious moment, all who live on the earth and believe in Jesus Christ will be purified and transformed completely to be with Him for all eternity.

Glorification changes our human form

In various places in this book is the quote that we are "fearfully and wonderfully made" (Psalm 139:14). There can be beauty in the human form. The physical, mental and creative talents of people can be remarkable. Such beauty, not just bodily beauty, illustrates the wonder of our creation by God. It can and should cause us to thank Him, as the Creator.

Youthfulness and young love often evidence the bodily beauty of the human form and the physical abilities of humankind. In the Song of Songs is written, "All beautiful you are, my darling; there is no flaw in you." (Song of Songs 4:7). Artists (visual, vocal, and actors), inventors, sportspeople and those with brilliant minds reveal the depth and breadth of skill embedded in the human form. Though it is proper to respect our human form and dignity, to care for it and protect it and to be thankful for it — it nonetheless will not last into heaven. Our earthly human form fades. It malfunctions. It becomes blemished and weak as we age. Our heavenly bodies will not be our earthly bodies. As previously discussed, our heavenly bodies will be spiritual bodies, yet with some characteristics and distinguishing features that identify our true, purified person. In heaven, we will be contemporaneously similar yet different from our earthly human form.

Glorification changes our human nature

Although scripture describes the beauty of the human form, how does scripture describe our inner nature? How is our core assessed and narrated? In scripture, people are variously described as:

(i)   incapacitated. We are unable to understand the things of God (1 Corinthians 2:14).
(ii) impure or stained (Jeremiah 2:22, Isaiah 1:16). We each are stained by the impurity of sin; failing to honour God, failing to truly love and care for those around us.
(iii) being lost (Isaiah 53:6). We like sheep are prone to go astray.
(iv) lawless (1 John 1:8; 1 John 3:4). We neither consistently nor strictly adhere to God's law. We err in thought and deed. We are not law-abiding; we occasionally or often knowingly break His law. We even define our humanity in terms of our propensity to err. We say "To err is human".
(v)   impaired (Isaiah 42:3). We are bruised and weakened. We are a smouldering wick rather than a glowing candle.
(vi) blind (2 Corinthians 4:4). We are blinded by ambition, avarice, envy, anger and vengeance. We fail to see the Light of Christ.
(vii) antagonistic or ambivalent. At times, by omission or rational choice we fail to do what is good, right or proper (John 3: 19).
(viii) enslaved (Romans 6:16-18). The apostle Paul is brutally and simply honest when he states that a person is either a slave to sin or a slave to God.
(ix) unrighteous (Hebrews 8:12). God is just. He always does the right thing. He is full of rightness. He is righteous. By contrast, we cannot and do not match by word or deed what is always just; what is right and proper. Legally, our behaviours and motivations lead us aptly to be judged as unrighteous. We are neither wholly nor fully right nor just in *all* our speaking, thinking and actions.

If such is our nature as listed above, then how can God who is pure and righteous welcome us into His presence? The simple and sufficient answer is that God, via His gospel (i.e. His good news), makes righteous those enabled to place their trust in Him. Motivated by His love for us, God sent His only Son, the Lord Jesus Christ, to be the means by which we ultimately can stand in God's presence. The apostle John wrote: "For God did not send his Son into the world to condemn the world, but to save the world through him." (John 3:17). The outcome of all that Christ did is that we can be welcomed into heaven. In Christ's own words "My Father's house has many rooms; if that were not so, would I have told you that I am going there to prepare a place for you? And if I go and prepare a place for you, I will come back and take you to be with me that you also may be where I am." (John 14:2-3). David in one of his psalms looks forward to heaven, saying, "in righteousness I shall see your face; when I awake, I shall be satisfied with seeing your likeness." (Psalm 17:15).

We, the unrighteous; He, our mantle of righteousness. We, the lost sheep; yet He, the good shepherd. We, the blind; He, the healing Light. We, the bruised; He, our protector and comforter. We, the law-breakers; He, the sinless fulfilment of the Law. We are stained and impure; He is the perfect unblemished Lamb of God.

Only the pure, the righteous enter heaven. The work of Christ and God's gift of faith enable those exercising that gift of faith to be made righteous, to be made acceptable to God and therefore, once purified, to stand in His presence. Hence, purification precedes and enables glorification. Our impurities are removed and our sinful earth-bound nature ends. In one of his letters, the apostle Peter writes, "we are looking forward to a new heaven and a new earth, the home of righteousness." (2 Peter 3:10,13). Heaven is the home of those made and judged righteous. To be righteous and enter into God's glorious presence requires the antecedent of purification. Purification removes legal uncleanness. 1 John 1:9 states, "If we confess our sins, he is faithful and just and will forgive us our sins and purify us from all unrighteousness." Similarly Isaiah 1:25b says of God's actions, "I will thoroughly purge away your dross and remove your impurities." and Ezekiel 36:25-27 says, "Then I will sprinkle clean water on you, and you shall be clean; I will cleanse you from all your filthiness and from all your idols. I will give you a new heart and put a new spirit within you; I will take the heart of stone out of your flesh and give you a heart of flesh. I will put My Spirit within you and cause you to walk in My statutes, and you will keep My judgments and do them." (NKJV). Lastly, the apostle Paul notes that; "if anyone is in Christ, he is a new creature; the old things passed away; behold, new things have come." (2 Corinthians 5:17).

Finally, to encourage personal reflection that helps fix eyes and hearts on the Lord God:

"Thus says the LORD: "Let not the wise man glory in his wisdom, Let not the mighty man glory in his might, Nor let the rich man glory in his riches;

But let him who glories glory in this, That he understands and knows Me, That I am the LORD, exercising lovingkindness, judgment, and righteousness in the earth. For in these I delight," says the LORD." (Jeremiah 9:23-24) (NKJV)

Bibliography

Barnes, A. (1962) *Barnes' notes on the New Testament*, (Ed: Ingram Cobbin), First American Reprint Edition, Kregel Publications, Grand Rapids, Michigan, USA.

Brand, C., Draper, C. and England, A. (Eds.) (1998) *Holman Illustrated Bible Dictionary*, Nashville: Holman Bible Publishers.

Brown C, (Ed.) (1971) *The New International Dictionary of the New Testament*, volume 2, Grand Rapids: Zondervan Publishing House.

Bruce, F.F. (1964) *The Epistle to the Hebrews*, NICNT/NLCNT, Grand Rapids, Michigan: Eerdmans.

Crosby. F. (1875) To God be the Glory. Lyrics by F. Crosby with tune by W.H. Doane, First published in *Brightest and Best: A Collection of New Songs for the Sunday School and Meetings of Prayer and Praise* by R. Lowry and W.H. Doane in 1875.

Edwards, J. (1844) *The Works of President Edwards in Four Volumes*, A reprint of the Worcester Edition, Leavitt, Trow and Co., 194 Broadway: New York and Wiley and Putnam: London.

Gaebelein, F.E. (Ed.) (1976) *The Expositor's Bible Commentary*, vol. 10 and 11, Grand Rapids: Zondervan Publishing House.

Hickman, E. (1840) The Works of Jonathan Edwards, A.M., Revised and corrected by Edward Hickman, Volume 1, Ball, Arnold and Co, 34 Paternoster Row, London.

Kirkpatrick, W.J. (1895) *Away in a Manger*. First published in Hewitt, E. E.; Sweeney, John R.; Kirkpatrick, Wm. J. (1895). *Around the World with Christmas: A Christmas Exercise*. Cincinnati: Cranston & Curts. p. 11.

Lewis, C.S. (1965) *The Weight of Glory*, C.S. Lewis, W.B. Eerdmans Publishing Company, Grand Rapids, Michigan, USA.

Lloyd-Jones, D.M. (1970) *Romans: Atonement and Justification*. Exposition of chapters 3:20-4:25, The Banner of Truth Trust, London, UK.

Lloyd-Jones, D.M. (1975) *Romans: An exposition of Chapter 8: 17-39*. The final perseverance of the Saints, Zondervan Publishing House, Grand Rapids, Michigan, USA.

Longman III, T. and Garland, D.E. (Eds) (2008) *The Expositor's Bible Commentary: Revised Edition*, Volume 11, Romans to Galatians, Zondervan, Grand Rapids, Michigan, USA.

MacLaren, A. (1904) *Expositions of Holy Scripture*. Hodder, London, UK.

Meyer, F.B. (1898) *Our Daily Homily*, Vol. 5: Matthew-Revelation (Classic Reprint), Forgotten Books, pp. 278.

Morgan, C.W. and Peterson, R.A. (Eds.) (2010) *The Glory of God*, Crossway, Wheaton, Illinois, USA.

Nicols, S.J. (2010) The Glory of God Present and Past, In *The Glory of God* (Eds: C.W. Morgan and R.A. Peterson), Wheaton, Illinois, USA.

Northrop, H.H. (2004) *The life and works of Charles Haddon Spurgeon*, Sword of the Lord Publishers, Murfreesboro, Tennessee, USA.

Pollock, J. (1969) *The Apostle: A Life of Saint Paul*, Hodder and Stoughton, UK.

Ryrie, C.C. (1990) *Transformed by His Glory*, Victor Books, Wheaton, Illinois, USA.

Spurgeon, C.H. (1883) Glory!, A sermon on May 20, 1883. Available at: https://www.spurgeon.org/resource-library/sermons/glory#flipbook/ [accessed 29 February, 2020]

Spurgeon, C.H. (1974) *Spurgeon's Devotional Bible*, Baker Book House Company, 6030 East Fulton Road, Ada, Michigan, USA.

Spurgeon, C.H. (1992) *Day by Day with C.H. Spurgeon*. Compiled by Al Bryant, Kregel Publications, Grand Rapids, Michigan, USA.

Spurgeon, C.H. *The Complete Works of C. H. Spurgeon*, Volume 29: Sermons 1698-1756, Delmarva Publications, Inc, Harrington, Delaware.

Spurgeon, C.H. *Sermon No 1721*, The Charles Spurgeon Sermon Collection (1834-1893). Available at https://www.thekingdomcollective.com/spurgeon/list/ [accessed 29 February, 2020]

Youngblood, R.F., Bruce, F.F. and Harrison, R.K. (Eds.) (1996) *Nelson's New Illustrated Bible Dictionary*, Nashville: Thomas Nelson Publishers.

Author Biography

Ross Kingwell is a professor of agricultural economics at the University of Western Australia. He is a distinguished fellow of the Australasian Agricultural and Resource Economics Society and chief economist in the Australian Export Grains Innovation Centre. However, as he readily admits, when it comes to theology or scripture, he heralds no formal qualification or academic prowess. Yet in spite of his amateur status, his study of the scripture, as revealed in this book, is nonetheless thorough, serious and insightful.

Printed in the United States
By Bookmasters